STAFFORDSHIRE LIBRARY AND INFORMATION SERVICES
Please return or renew by the last date shown

13. OCT 11.

1 3 MAY 2013
29/9/14

If not required by other readers, this item may be renewed in person, by post or telephone, online or by email.
To renew, either the book or ticket are required

24 HOUR RENEWAL LINE 0845 33 00 740

D1333452

ROBIN HOOD

'It is as if we were viewing the whole sequence of events from an immense distance; we can see the action but we cannot identify the actors, and because they are out of earshot we can judge them only by what they do'
Maurice Keen, *The Outlaws of Medieval Legend* (1961)

'*Oliver.* Where will the old duke live?
Charles. They say he is already in the forest of Arden, and a many merry men with him; and there they live like the old Robin Hood of England: they say many young gentlemen flock to him every day, and fleet the time carelessly, as they did in the golden world.'
William Shakespeare, *As You Like It*, Act 1, Scene 1.

ROBIN HOOD

The English Outlaw Unmasked

DAVID
BALDWIN

AMBERLEY

First published 2010

Amberley Publishing Plc
Cirencester Road, Chalford,
Stroud, Gloucestershire, GL6 8PE

www.amberley-books.com

ISBN 978 1 84868 378 5

British Library Cataloguing in Publication
Data.

A catalogue record for this book is available
from the British Library.

Typeset in 11pt on 12pt Sabon.
Typesetting by FONTHILLDESIGN.
Printed in the UK.

CONTENTS

PREFACE

Robin Hood, the brilliant archer who 'robbed the rich to give to the poor' and who always triumphed over the forces of evil really needs no introduction, but the man behind the legend is as mysterious as King Arthur. There were outlaws who lived in the royal forests preying on unwary travellers, and Robin Hoods whose names are recorded in historical documents: but no one has been able to prove that one of these real Robins was the individual whose exploits were commemorated in ballad and song.

One reason why researchers have failed to find the historical Robin Hood is that many of them have been looking in the wrong time and for the wrong person. No chronicler claimed to know Robin the famous outlaw, and there is evidence that Robin – or Robert – Hood – or Hod or Hude – was a nickname given to petty criminals from at least the middle of the thirteenth century. It may be no coincidence that Robin is very close to 'robbing', and that there are still 'hoodies' who seek to intimidate by obscuring their features. The man whose deeds inspired the legend may not have been called Robin Hood from birth and perhaps not even in his own lifetime. Mass-media and the rapid dissemination of information are a comparatively recent phenomenon, and the tales undoubtedly grew with the telling. We need to look for someone whose opposition to perceived injustice was admired by his contemporaries and whose career is reflected in the earliest ballads.

The starting point for all Robin Hood studies remains Sir James Holt's *Robin Hood* (second edition, 1989), notwithstanding the publication of Stephen Knight's *Robin Hood: A Complete Study of the English Outlaw* five years later. Knight is a literary scholar, and although his work contains a number of valuable insights he has little time for the historical Robin. Writers like John Bellamy, J.R. Maddicott, and, more recently, A.J. Pollard have tried to bridge the gap between myth and reality, and have increased our understanding in the process: but Robin, Little John, and their great enemy the Sheriff of Nottingham, remain as elusive as ever.

Selection of material is always necessary, and seldom more so than when dealing with the Robin Hood ballads. I have decided to quarry only those that were undoubtedly in existence by the end of the fifteenth century, although some that survive only in later copies may have equally long pedigrees. *The Jolly Pinder of Wakefield*, and *Robin Hood and the Curtal Friar* (to note just two examples), were almost certainly popular long before they were written down in the mid-seventeenth century, but the further the stories are removed from the Middle Ages, the less reliable their historical content. They must be used with caution at all times.

I first became interested in Robin Hood when a friend lent me a copy of Maurice Keen's *The Outlaws of Medieval Legend* in the 1960s. I returned to him from time to time over the years, and when I began to teach included him in a course entitled 'Mysteries of History' and in a University of Leicester 'summer holiday week'. I would like to thank Jonathan Reeve at Amberley Publishing for suggesting that I undertake a fuller, more accessible, study, Mary E. Robertson, Chief Curator of Manuscripts at the Huntington Library, San Marino, for checking references to the Godberds in the Hastings family archive, Lesley Boatwright and Tina Hampson for help with transcribing and translating documents, David Hepworth and Rob Lynley for sharing the results of their own research into Roger Godberd with me, and my wife Joyce who spent holidays looking for Robin Hood connections in obscure locations and helped in many other ways. Their contributions have been invaluable, but any mistakes are entirely my own.

David Baldwin, December 2009

PROLOGUE:
ROBIN HOOD'S WORLD

Whoever Robin Hood was, and whenever, precisely, he lived, he would have been as much part of, and influenced by, the nature of his surroundings as we are by ours. His life cannot be separated from his 'times' because without those times there would have been no famous outlaw, only a man who lived and died largely unnoticed and who was quickly forgotten. Robin's world was essentially the world of the thirteenth century, a world dominated by kings, lords and churchmen but sustained by the sweat and toil of peasants. The ballads describe him as a yeoman, a small, independent farmer, and his attitudes were those of his class.

Robin's society was essentially feudal. Everyone who held land held it of someone who ultimately, held of the king, and the reigning king was his own prime minister and commander-in-chief. He was assisted – and sometimes obstructed – by around a dozen earls, a larger number of barons, and by senior churchmen whose literary skills and membership of the Church universal made them ideal administrators and ambassadors. Beneath them were knights and squires, various degrees of lesser clergy, middle class lawyers and merchants, yeomen, and, at the base of the pyramid, the unfree peasants. Peasants were tied to their manors, subject to the regulations of the manorial court, and obliged to work on their lord's land for two or three days a week. They could not abscond because, by and large, there was nowhere to run to – full employment meant that no one would have hired them or given them refuge if they had.

Medieval people believed that the ordering of society had been determined by God and was fixed and unalterable. The secular aristocracy fought to protect everyone (at least in theory), the clergy prayed for everyone, and the peasants toiled in the fields so that everyone could eat. These basic assumptions held good for much of the Middle Ages (at least until after the Great Rebellion of 1381), but nothing was ever quite as unchanging as was sometimes supposed. The population, which had stood at perhaps one and a half millions when Domesday Book was compiled in 1086, had grown to approximately three millions by the late thirteenth century, mainly thanks to an improving standard of living (resulting in a higher birth rate), and the development of a money economy. Individuals and the nation as a whole were less dependent on what could be grown in a particular year, but the expectation of life was still only half of what it is nowadays. If a man survived childhood and avoided a fatal illness or accident in early manhood he might live to be seventy or even eighty; but he entered old age soon after fifty and by sixty-five would have buried most of his friends.

The growing population and rising living standards were clear signs that England was becoming wealthier, a change also reflected in the development of a thriving trade in imports and exports that had scarcely existed before 1066. English merchants sent wool to Flanders, herrings to Gascony, and corn to Norway, and in return received not only cloth, wine and timber but precious stones and spices the merchants of Italy brought from the Middle and Far

East. The thirteenth century was the era of the 'Pax Mongolica', the 'Mongol Peace'. Genghis Khan's conquests had torn down the barrier that had divided the East from the West for centuries, and eastern goods reached Europe in hitherto unprecedented quantities while the Mongol Empire lasted. No English trader rivalled Marco Polo, but suppliers and their customers seized the opportunity while it was there.

The people who stood to benefit most from the new prosperity were the nobles, but their gains were modified in practice by the rise of the 'gentry' and by the fact that the baronial share of the riches was concentrated in increasingly fewer hands. Edward I may have deliberately tried to reduce the number of earldoms, partly as a way of enriching junior members of the royal family, but equally because he preferred to deal with fewer powerful and potentially over-mighty subjects.[1] Most barons had incomes from land of between £100 and £500 per annum, but the leading earls were worth between £1,000 and £2,000 – enough to make them millionaires by contemporary reckonings. Henry III's brother, Richard of Cornwall, could single-handedly reform the currency and shore up the Crown's finances, and Simon de Montfort was always pre-occupied with money. Disputes over his wife's dower from her first husband plagued his relations with Henry for many years.

Income was crucial of course, but the goodwill of the king was equally important if an earl or baron hoped to prosper. One reason was that entry fines – the sums paid by heirs for the right to 'enter' i.e. inherit, their late fathers' properties – were often fixed at arbitrary levels and could be enforced or rescinded at the royal will. A powerful lord who enjoyed the king's favour might never pay more than a fraction of his obligation, and although the king was unlikely to demand an annual instalment which exceeded that which could reasonably be afforded, it is worth noting that in 1230 some sixty per cent of the barons were burdened by these recurring and ever-present debts. This did not make them royal sycophants – the king was often as much in debt as they were – but it ensured that they looked increasingly to the patronage of the court.

Some changes were more helpful, however. The break-up of the post-Conquest knights fees (the arrangement by which feudal tenants held their estates), allowed the aristocracy to substitute fines for military service, and mercenaries became the backbone of the royal army.[2] The great lords built larger, more sophisticated castles incorporating comfortable dwelling houses with hangings, rugs and glass for the windows – still primitive by our standards but far more luxurious than the eleventh and twelfth-century keeps. There also developed the largesse, the public display of wealth and generosity, which became as much as yardstick of chivalric conduct as knightly combat and participation in tournaments. The tournament replaced war as the warriors' favourite occupation during the late twelfth and thirteenth centuries, the original melees or free-for-alls giving way to jousting and individual combat between armed knights. They still made a virtue of violence, but the violence was controlled and less likely to result in fatal or serious injury. Ladies 'favours', which became the object of the contests, also helped to soften their image, and the Church did not object to a practice which prepared men for that worthiest of all challenges, the crusade.

The crusades were a series of military expeditions designed to recover Jerusalem and the Holy Land from the Muslims initiated by Pope Urban II in 1096. The first of these was dramatically successful, but Jerusalem was again lost in 1187 and little was accomplished thereafter. Richard the Lionheart's Third Crusade regained some ground in the early 1190s and the Emperor Frederick took advantage of wars between the Muslim powers to secure access to Jerusalem for ten years in 1227; but King St Louis was decisively defeated in Egypt in 1248, and when he died at Tunis in 1270 the ideal all but died with him. The problem was that the logistical difficulties – and the cost – of mounting a crusade meant that such enterprises could only be undertaken periodically, and it became difficult to harness enthusiasm for what must have seemed a dangerous, as well as an increasingly lost, enterprise. Christians believed their cause enjoyed divine approval, but the God of battles seemed to be fighting for Islam.

Sending knights on an 'armed pilgrimage' (as the crusade was euphemistically termed), obliged the Church to adjust its traditional attitude towards warfare, and there were changes in other areas too. The days when great lords founded monasteries were already passing, but in their place an increasing number of lesser men endowed chantries while cathedrals and abbeys reaped the benefit of higher incomes derived from their tithes and extensive properties. The new money was not evenly distributed, however. The two archbishops and the bishops of Winchester, Ely and Durham had incomes equal to those of the wealthiest earls, and maintained palaces, employed retinues and displayed their generosity on a comparable scale: but at the same time there were poor bishops in Wales who were permitted to hold an English deanery to supplement their local revenues and who would not have supposed that they were working for the richest institution in the world. Royal servants and men engaged in teaching in the rising universities who were increasingly supported by religious preferment were almost permanently absent from their livings; the monastic orders had lost much of their original fervour; and even the papacy was beginning to forfeit some of its former prestige as it grew increasingly powerful and became ever more involved in war and politics. But the thirteenth century still produced an unusually high number of distinguished bishops; saw Oxford and Cambridge flourish and nurture some of the finest scholars; saw the arrival of the friars and the introduction of the ideals of St Francis and St Dominic into England; and witnessed the development of Gothic architecture – the flowering of the Early English style and the beginnings of the Decorated. There were losses, but there were gains too.

Ordinary people had few opportunities to 'better' themselves but the growth in commerce meant that more found employment in urban industries and townsmen became an increasingly important element in society. London became the seat of royal government (which was becoming ever more elaborate and complex), and Londoners a political force in the land. By the thirteenth century the ruling oligarchy of mayor and aldermen was firmly established, and the city was steadily augmenting its privileges and attaining the communal identity which allowed it to influence national politics. Control of the capital and the support of its leading citizens became increasingly vital to any cause.

The peasants are the silent class in medieval society, silent because they were wholly illiterate and could leave no records of their own. A fortunate few who prospered built up substantial smallholdings; but life for the majority remained hard and comfortless, and the growing demand for food (to feed a rising population), meant that the pressures on them to work longer and produce more had never been greater. They were a 'commodity', to be bought, sold and used as the owner of an estate chose, but were often more inclined to be truculent than subservient. The knives they carried to perform a host of daily tasks were soon drawn when they became angry, and many a peasant found himself accused not only of taking a life but of destroying his master's property. The law did not recognize what we today call manslaughter – the accused could not claim that he did not mean to kill or that the death was an accident – and the only excuse available to him was to maintain that he had acted in self-defence i.e. that his victim would have murdered him if he had not struck first. It is hardly surprising that those brought before the courts invariably argued that this was indeed what had happened, or that judges were inclined to accept what was inevitably a one-sided argument. Hanging the offender would only have doubled the lord's loss![3]

We have talked almost exclusively about men this far because this was a male dominated society. Women had their place as wives, mothers and homemakers, but they could not sue in court – or even make a will – without their husband's approval. Any lands they possessed were administered by, and effectively belonged to, their spouses, but they came into their own in two particular areas. One was that they were expected to deputize for their lord if he happened to be away from home for any reason, and the other was to use their personal relationship with him to intercede for plaintiffs and seek to mitigate his intrinsic male harshness. Most of the wives we can glimpse seem to have fulfilled these duties successfully, and a few may even have 'worn the trousers' behind the scenes.

This then was Robin Hood's world, a world dominated by the rich and powerful who held the vast majority in thrall. Most people's lives were short and hard and death was always imminent, but they knew how to enjoy themselves and to seize their opportunities. It was, in one sense, an immoral world – gain usually took precedence over any concept of right or wrong – and justice was always arbitrary. Rape, for example, might be frowned upon, but only because it had devalued the victim as future wife for someone, not because of the hurt she would have suffered. If there was a basic assumption, it was that everyone ought to look after him or her-self. The medieval state did not concern itself with the well-being of its citizens, and those who became ill or who fell on hard times could only hope that their lord, or perhaps the local abbey, would show them some compassion. Chivalry, with its high-minded concepts, applied only to those who were members of the same chivalric, i.e. aristocratic, class in society, and did not require the great and the good to treat their peasants with anything other than their usual severity. All in all it was an uncompromising world, one in which a low-born rebel who defied the norms could readily become a hero to those who would have done likewise if only they had dared.

I

TALES OF ROBIN HOOD

Robin Hood is so popular, and seems so real to a modern day audience, that it is hard to believe that some writers have questioned his very existence. Surely, the outlaw portrayed so convincingly by Errol Flynn and Richard Greene is more than a figment of a medieval minstrel's imagination, and surely too, Little John and the Sheriff of Nottingham were more than fictitious characters invented to fight the battle between good and evil? The answer is a cautious 'yes', although they were undoubtedly men whose story grew from small beginnings. They did not become heroes or villains instantly – later generations accorded them that status – but they and their activities are discernible in medieval documents if we discard the popular images and begin our search with open minds.

Historians have argued that Robin Hood could have lived at any time between the early thirteenth and the first quarter of the fourteenth centuries, but we have no detailed account of him until the earliest ballads emerge 100 years later. Of these, the longest, and possibly also the oldest, is the *Little Geste of Robyn Hode and his Meiny* (i.e. followers), a work of 456 four-line stanzas, divided into eight cantos, or 'fyttes'. It is not a single poem but rather a compilation of five others, *Robin Hood and the Knight*, *Robin Hood and the Sheriff*, *Little John and the Sheriff*, *Robin Hood and the King*, and *Robin Hood his Death*, blended together to tell a more or less continuous story.[1] The action begins, rather abruptly, in Barnsdale, in Yorkshire, in early summer, with Little John asking Robin how the outlaws should live and who they should rob. Robin tells him not to harm hard-working husbandmen and yeomen or even knights and squires who would be 'good fellows', but to show no mercy to the rich and unjust:

> These bisshoppes and these archebisshoppes,
> Ye shall them bete and bynde;
> The hye sherif of Notyingham,
> Hym holde ye in your mynde.

We are not told how Robin became an outlaw, how he formed his band, or gang, or why, if he was living in Yorkshire, he was so bitterly opposed to the Sheriff of Nottingham. He was a man with a 'past', but a past the storyteller did not choose to relate.

Robin sends Little John, Will Scarlok (Scarlett), and Much the Miller's son up 'the Sayles' to Watling Street to find a guest to share their dinner, 'guest' meaning a wealthy traveller who will be relieved of his money after he has dined. They meet a knight, not a well-equipped warrior but a man who, from his 'symple aray' and downcast expression, has clearly fallen on hard times. He agrees to share their meal, but is found to have only the meagre (for a knight) sum of ten shillings in his pocket. The reason, he explains, is that his son has killed a knight of Lancaster and he has mortgaged his lands to the Abbot of St Mary's, York, to raise £400 to save his life. Some friends who he hoped would help him repay the debt have deserted him, and he is on his way to York to beg the abbot to allow him more time to raise the money. Robin listens sympathetically and decides to help him. He is given £400 from the outlaws' own coffers, together with new clothes, horse, harness and Little John to serve him. The only security he can offer is to invoke the name of Our Lady, but Robin accepts his promise that he will repay the loan in a year's time.

The knight and Little John ride on to St Mary's where the abbot and the justice he has bribed to assist him, gleefully await their arrival. The knight goes through the motions of pleading for more time to pay (knowing, of course, that they will refuse him), and in their moment of triumph throws the £400 down on the table before them. The abbot is so dumbfounded that he is unable to finish his dinner, and his mood is not improved when the justice refuses to return the now useless bribe. He cannot even ask the knight for a 'favour', a gift that would have compensated for the interest no Christian was allowed to charge.

A year later, the knight has saved enough money to repay Robin's loan, and sets out for Barnsdale well equipped and with 100 bowmen in his retinue. On the way he stumbles upon a country fair where a wrestling match is in progress. Several valuable prizes, a white bull, a courser, a pipe of wine and other items, are won by a stranger, and this so angers some of the 'locals' that they decide to kill him. The knight intervenes, and after he has given the man his dues he pacifies any lingering ill-feeling by buying the wine from him and 'standing' all those present a drink.

The scene now switches to Nottingham where Little John is preparing to shoot in the sheriff's archery contest. He wins, of course, and the sheriff, greatly impressed, invites him to enter his service. John accepts on condition that the sheriff first obtains his current master's, i.e. the knight's, permission, and agrees to work for him (using the alias Reynold Greenleaf of Holderness), for twelve months. One Wednesday, John demands his dinner before the sheriff returns from hunting, and this leads to a violent quarrel with the cook. They exchange blows for an hour by which time they have earned one another's respect, and John invites the cook to join the outlaws. That night, they steal away taking the sheriff's plate and £300 in cash with them. John then seeks out the sheriff (who has not returned home and is unaware of what has happened), and tells him that he knows where deer are to be found. But it is just a trick to betray him to the outlaws. The unhappy man is taken to their camp where he has to eat venison served on his own plate and dress in Lincoln green before spending an uncomfortable night in the forest. He is released only after promising not to harass Robin in future, and is 'charged' £300, (the £300 already stolen by Little John and the cook), for his meal.

In fytte four Robin again sends Little John, Will and Much to Watling Street to 'invite' a suitable 'guest' to join them for dinner. They apprehend two monks from St Mary's Abbey who are found to have £800 in their saddlebags, exactly double the amount borrowed by the knight. The knight has by now extricated himself from the wrestling match, and when he arrives at the outlaws' camp Robin tells him that the monks[2] have paid his debt for him. He also gives him the second £400, and this part of the story ends happily.

So far the mood has been gentle. The sheriff and the monks have lost some of their wealth and suffered embarrassment, but there has been no bloodshed or violence. All this is about to change, however. The outlaws, confident that they will not now be molested, decide to go to Nottingham to compete in the

Geste's second archery contest. Robin wins the prize of the silver arrow, but no sooner has he done so than the sheriff reneges on his promise and orders his men to attack. A sharp fight ensues in which Little John is wounded, and he, Robin and the others seek refuge in the friendly knight's castle, described as being 'double dyched' and lying 'a lytell within the wode'. The knight, who is now identified as Sir Richard at the Lee, raises the drawbridge, and tells the pursuing sheriff that he will surrender the fugitives to no one but the King. The sheriff goes to London where the King assures him that he will deal with both Robin and Sir Richard when he comes northwards in two weeks time, but the former decides to leave nothing to chance. On his return to Nottingham he ambushes Sir Richard who is hawking by the river, and orders that he be taken to the city and executed. But the outlaws (who have now returned to the greenwood), are alerted by the knight's wife, and mount a rescue as he is being taken to the gallows. The sheriff is pierced by an arrow before being beheaded, and Robin and the freed Sir Richard return to their forest lair.

The King is angry when he learns of what has happened, and his fury knows no bounds when he sees at first hand how the outlaws have poached his deer in Plumpton Park, near Knaresborough. He offers all Sir Richard's lands to anyone who will betray the miscreants, but there are no takers. One of his servants suggests that, if he wants to confront Robin, he has only to ride into the forest dressed as a rich monk accompanied by a few followers. The stratagem works, and the King soon finds himself in the outlaws' camp. His worst fears are confirmed when he is relieved of half the £40 he has with him, but the mood changes dramatically when he produces a letter summoning Robin to Nottingham. Robin immediately recognizes the royal seal attached to it, and declares that he loves the King, its owner, better than any man in the world. The 'monks' are entertained to dinner followed by an archery contest in which the losers forfeit their equipment and receive a buffeting. When Robin himself misses, he asks the 'abbot' to give him a buffet, and the force of the blow makes him realize that this is no ordinary churchman. He recognizes the King, and he, Sir Richard, and all the outlaws fall on their knees before him. The King forgives them on condition that Robin and his men abandon their life in the forest and enter his service. He puts on Lincoln green as a gesture of goodwill, and they all ride to Nottingham shooting as they go.

Robin serves the King for a year or more, but by then only Little John and Will Scarlett are still with him and he begins to yearn for his old haunts in the forest. He obtains permission to visit a chapel he has founded in Barnsdale, but then goes absent without leave and summons his 'yonge men' to rejoin him. Some twenty-two years pass, and Robin, who is now old and ailing, decides to go to Kirklees Priory, near Huddersfield, to be bled by his kinswoman, the prioress. Will and the other outlaws fear treachery, but Robin disregards them and takes only Little John with him. The *Geste* devotes only a few lines to Robin's death, but other, fragmentary, versions of the story tell of how he was excessively bled by the prioress and then set upon by her lover, Red Roger or Sir Roger of Doncaster. We are not told why Robin is at loggerheads with these two: only that although he kills Roger, he is mortally wounded in the process, and by the time Little John hears the commotion it is too late. Robin refuses to let John burn the priory in retaliation, and with his last ounce of strength shoots an arrow to mark the spot where he wishes to be buried.

There are three other ballads, or stories, of Robin that can be dated to the fifteenth century, *Robin Hood and the Potter, Robin*

Hood and Guy of Gisborne, and *Robin Hood and the Monk.* The first of these, the *Potter,* mirrors the gentle mood of the first part of the *Geste,* but the other two are much fiercer. The potter in question often passes through the outlaws' territory, but refuses to pay pavage, a toll levied on road use, for the privilege. Little John has already been worsted by him, and when Robin tries to intercept him he fares no better. They become friends however, and Robin persuades him to allow him to adopt his identity and sell his wares in Nottingham. His 'cut-price' stall attracts a large crowd, and when Robin generously gives the last of the pots to the sheriff's wife she asks him to dine at her husband's table. There, everyone is talking about an archery contest which has been arranged, and Robin, naturally, competes and wins the prize. He tells the sheriff that he learned his skills from Robin Hood himself, and readily agrees to take him to 'Robin' in the greenwood. Of course, no sooner are they in the forest than Robin blows his horn and the sheriff is captured. The unfortunate man is forced to surrender his horse and everything he has with him in return for a white palfrey, a gift from Robin to his wife. He rides back to Nottingham a laughing-stock, and Robin gives the potter £10, three times the value of his pots.

Robin Hood and Guy of Gisborne begins with Robin dreaming of two yeomen who set upon and injure him. The vision is so real that he decides to look for them, but just as he and Little John catch sight of what appears to be one of them, they quarrel and go their separate ways. The man is Guy of Gisborne, an old enemy of Robin's, who the sheriff has hired to capture or kill him. They do not immediately recognize one another however, and it is only after a shooting match (which Robin wins), that they identify themselves and fall to blows. Guy is slain, and Robin cuts off his head, disfigures it, and spikes it on the end of his bow. He then puts on Guy's jacket, pulling the hood well over his features, and blows a loud blast on the dead man's horn.

Little John has meanwhile returned to Barnsdale where he stumbles on the bodies of two fellow outlaws and sees Will Scarlett being hotly pursued by the sheriff. He intervenes to save Will, but his bow breaks in his hand leaving him defenceless. The sheriff threatens him with summary execution, but no sooner has he been tied to a tree than Robin sounds Guy's horn. Guy has told the sheriff that he will blow the horn to signal that he has killed Robin, and the sheriff is in no doubt that it is Guy who now comes striding towards him. He offers him any favour he would care to ask, and is puzzled when 'Guy' asks permission to kill the bound Little John there and then. All Robin does, of course, is to cut his comrade's bonds, pressing Guy's bow into his hands as he does so, and the sheriff is shot and killed as he and his men flee.

The third ballad, *Robin Hood and the Monk*, opens similarly. Robin is concerned that he has not heard mass for some time, and decides to visit St Mary's Church in Nottingham. He agrees to take Little John with him, but they again quarrel and John returns to Sherwood. During the mass Robin is recognized by a 'gret-hedid munke' who slips out to alert the sheriff, and is seized after defending himself against impossible odds. Fortunately, a well-wisher who has seen what has happened tells the outlaws, and they plan a rescue. The monk who raised the alarm is sent to carry word of Robin's capture to the King, but as he nears the forest he falls in with two yeomen who offer to help him avoid Robin's band. The yeomen are Little John and Much, and when they reach a secluded place they behead both the monk and the 'litull page' who accompanies him. After hiding the bodies, they take the letters the monk was carrying to the King who makes them yeomen of the Crown with a fee of £20 and sends them back to Nottingham with instructions to bring Robin to him in person. The sheriff invites them to stay in his house when they tell him they are deputizing for the monk because the King has appointed him Abbot of Westminster; and when everyone is asleep they quietly kill the porter, use his keys to let Robin out of prison, and are safe in the greenwood by dawn. The sheriff fears for his life and position for allowing Robin to escape; but the King has to admit that he, too, has been duped and (in this ballad), they all live to fight another day.

It is immediately apparent that although these stories are quite separate, they have a number of common themes, or motifs, running through them. Only *Robin Hood and the Monk* lacks an archery contest, and disguise, or their enemies' failure to recognize them, is central to the outlaws' success. Robin places himself in danger by taking only Little John with him to Kirklees in the *Geste* and to Nottingham in the *Monk*, and he and John quarrel and part company in both the *Monk* and in *Guy of Gisborne*. Robin is worsted by, and then befriends, the potter just as Little John fights and then joins forces with the sheriff's cook in the *Geste*, and Robin's entry into royal service in the *Geste* is comparable with the reward given to Little John and Much in the *Monk*. Robin is misunderstood by the King although he is impeccably loyal to him, a loyalty mirrored in his devotion to Our Lady noticed in both the *Geste* and the *Monk*. They are traditional tales in which the heroes (and the audience), are always one step ahead of the villains, and in which the villains usually get their just desserts.

The earliest mention of the ballads is in William Langland's *The Vision of Piers Plowman* (c.1377), where the negligent priest Sloth says: 'I kan noght parfitly my *Paternoster* as the preest it syngeth,

But I kan rymes of Robyn Hood and Randolf Erl of Chestre.'³ The only thirteenth-century Randolf (more usually Ranulf), Earl of Chester, was Ranulf 'de Blundeville' (i.e. of Oswestry), who died in 1232, but it is unclear if he was associated with Robin in some way, or whether, alternatively, there were two separate 'rymes' or ballad cycles. Chaucer alludes to Robin, without specifically naming him, in *Troilus and Criseyde* (1380), and a fragment of verse scribbled in a Lincoln Cathedral manuscript of *c.*1410 notes that 'Robyn hod in scherewod stod, hodud [hooded] and hathud [hatted] and hosut [hosed] and schod'.⁴ The priestly author of the homiletic *Dives and Pauper*, written at about the same time, complains that people would rather 'hear a tale or a song of Robin Hood or of some ribaldry' than go to mass or matins, and it was not long before contemporary outlaws were emulating his deeds. In 1439 a gang led by one Piers Venables rescued a prisoner and then took refuge in the forest 'like as it hadde be Robyn Hode and his meyne', and two years later a group of yeomen and labourers who blocked the road in South Acre, Norfolk, and threatened to murder Sir Geoffrey Harsyk sang 'we are Robynhodesmen, war, war, war.'⁵ Sir John Paston's complaint that a servant he had 'kepyd thys iij [three] yer to pleye Seynt Jorge and Robyn Hod and the Shryff of Notyngham' had left him shows that the stories were popular in Norfolk by the third quarter of the fifteenth century;⁶ and Bishop Hugh Latimer found he could not compete with Robin when he went to preach at a certain church shortly before 1549. He said:

> I tarried there half an houer and more, [until] at last the key was founde, and one of the parishe commes to me and sayes, 'Syr, thys is a busye daye with us, we can not heare you, it is Robin hoods daye'... It is no laughynge matter my friends, it is a weepyng matter,

a heavy matter, under the pretence of gatherynge for Robin Hood, a traytourer, and a thefe, to put out a preacher, to have hys office less esteemed... [7]

So does this mean that the earliest ballads came into being some little time before 1377, and did not exist say, fifty or a hundred years earlier? Not at all. Professor Holt has pointed out that French and Anglo-Norman became foreign tongues after the Cornish scholar John Trevisa (1342–1402), revised the literary syllabus at Oxford, and 'the result was to create a cultural desert which was rapidly filled by the extraordinary blossoming of English as a literary language from the middle of the fourteenth century.'[8] Langland, Chaucer and Sir Thomas Mallory could not have penned their masterpieces in the intellectual milieu of the thirteenth century, and peasants, and perhaps even knights, would always have enjoyed listening to good stories told in their own everyday language. The ballads may not have been committed to writing until after 1377, but versions of them, learned by heart and passed from one minstrel to another, could have been circulating many years before.

There are many other tales and accounts of Robin whose origins are later than the fifteenth century, and the modern version of the story had been heavily influenced by them. The idea that he 'robbed the rich to give to the poor' is perhaps foreshadowed in the *Geste's* closing comment that he 'did poor men much good', but it was the Scottish historian John Major who, in 1521, wrote that 'he permitted no harm to women, nor seized the goods of the poor, but helped them generously with what he took from abbots'.[9] The men who, in the earliest ballads, fought with cooks and potters were not always well-disposed towards those in their own class in society, and their much vaunted piety did not deter them from mutilating enemies and killing children. None of them seems to have a home, or a wife, or children, and even Maid Marian, the essential romantic element in today's story, was not associated with the outlaw Robin until the seventeenth century. Alexander Barclay, a pre-Reformation monk, connects them in a single sentence – 'some may fit of Maide Marian, or els of Robin Hood' – but their traditions were then quite separate. It was the minstrels who brought them together, not love.[10]

The Robin they sang about was a yeoman, but in later stories he became a dispossessed nobleman. John Leland, writing in the 1530s, refers to him as a *'nobilis exlex'*, a noble outlaw, meaning, in all probability, that he was high minded. But the word 'noble' also has aristocratic connotations, and Richard Grafton claimed in 1569 that he had found evidence that this was indeed the case:

> In an olde and auncient Pamphlet I finde this written of the sayd Robert Hood. This man (sayth he) discended of a noble parentage: or rather being of a base stocke and linage, was for his manhoode and chivalry advanced to the noble dignitie of an Erle, excelling principally in Archery, or shootyng, his manly courage agreeing therunto.[11]

The pamphlet, whatever it was, has long since vanished, and it goes without saying that Robin could not have been 'of base stocke' if he had been born to noble parents. It is unlikely that an earl would have been outlawed for falling into debt or would have 'gathered together a companye of Roysters and Cutters' as Grafton claims later, but these objections did not prevent the Tudor writer Anthony Munday from popularizing the idea in his plays, *The Downfall of*

Robert, Earl of Huntington, and *The Death of Robert, Earl of Huntington,* in 1598. Martin Parker's *A True Tale of Robin Hood* (1632) stated unequivocally that the 'renowned outlaw, Robert Earl of Huntington, vulgarly called Robin Hood, lived and died in AD 1198, being the ninth year of the reign of King Richard the First'; but the real Earl of Hunting*don* (the only possible interpretation of Hunting*ton*), was David of Scotland, who died in 1219. A prose life of Robin preserved in a manuscript in the Sloane collection in the British Library adds the detail that he was born at Locksley (Loxley), three miles north-west of Sheffield, and he was called 'Locksley' (or 'Robin of Locksley') in a late ballad, *Robin Hood and Queen Katherine,* and in Sir Walter Scott's *Ivanhoe,* published in 1820. Scott's Robin was a latter-day Anglo-Saxon who opposed the depredations of the Norman conquerors; but legal records seldom distinguish between 'Saxon' and 'Norman' after 1200 implying that the two peoples were fast assuming a shared identity. A good story mattered more than the facts.

Who were these outlaws? They were just a handful of perhaps thousands of individuals who were charged – or who thought they were about to be charged – with felonies, and who fled rather than submit to trial. They would forfeit their goods and lands (if they had any), and would be executed if captured;[12] but there were no policemen in the Middle Ages, and both the will and the means to deal with them were lacking. Occasionally, a local worthy might be commissioned to pursue a particularly notorious criminal, but in most cases the outlaw simply 'disappeared' into another area. It was unlikely that his past would catch up with him if he led a subsequently blameless life.

Modern films and novels have often portrayed Robin as a *leader* of the discontented, but there is no hint of this in the earliest stories. He resists the sheriff and some churchmen because they are corrupt and unjust, but does not resent them because their lives are more comfortable than those of the peasantry. The forest outlaws also wanted to live well and make money, but they did not seek to change the way society was ordered. When problems arose, their only solution, as Maurice Keen has pointed out, was 'the same court with a different judge and a different jury', and it is no coincidence that loyalty to the king – and the system he represented – is one of Robin's most striking characteristics in the ballads.

> It was only in an imaginary England that an ideal hero could emerge triumphant from his defiance of the injustice of the system, and, by rounding off the careers of a few corrupt officials in a splendid victory for retributive justice, usher in a new dispensation in which the poor man obtained his due from the harsh world.[13]

Robin's base, the outlaws' raison d'être in the ballads, was the forest, more specifically the large areas of woodland that Norman and later kings had made their private hunting grounds. The harsh laws that protected these royal forests were bitterly resented by those who were denied access to them, and their repeal was one of the reforms demanded by the peasant leader Wat Tyler as late as 1381. It follows that those who resisted this 'injustice', who cocked a snook at authority by living in the forests and poaching the venison, would become heroes to ordinary people, and there would have been many whose careers mirrored Robin's even if they were called by other names.

But was life on the run really so carefree, or were Tyler and his friends harking back to a golden age that had never existed? The forests would have been an ideal lair in summer when the weather was warm, the vegetation thick, and the food plentiful, but what about winter when it was cold and wet and the trees were leafless? There would have been few pickings when the greenery no longer hid Robin and those like him from unwary travellers, and when they themselves were more likely to be seen and captured. It may seem trite to suggest that being an outlaw was a 'seasonal' occupation, but there is every likelihood that the 'merry men' spent the harsher months of the year in their own homes or with friends and relatives. It is always summer in the ballads – perhaps it had to be!

2

MYTH & REALITY

The early ballads tell us more about Robin Hood and his band than any other source of information, but how historically reliable are they? We have to remember that their purpose was to entertain contemporaries, not to inform historians, and whatever facts they contained at the beginning would have been obscured as new layers of meaning were added. Much of the story they tell is traditional, based on earlier tales of older outlaws; but equally, there are allusions and statements that chime accurately with real events and real people. A legend has to begin or originate with *something*, however much it is subsequently changed.

The first outlaw whose exploits – both real and legendary – influenced the Robin Hood cycle was Hereward, usually surnamed 'the Wake'. All that is really known of him is that he held lands of two abbeys, Croyland and Peterborough, and in 1070 joined in a Danish attack on the latter, ostensibly to deprive the new Norman abbot of its treasures. After the Danes left he retired to Ely where he resisted attempts to dislodge him and from where he escaped with a few followers when the island was captured the following summer. Many stories were subsequently told of him, and it can hardly be coincidence that in one episode he decides to spy out the Norman camp and persuades a potter to lend him his pots as a disguise. The similarity between this and Robin selling borrowed pots to the sheriff's wife in Nottingham is obvious, and the pattern continues when he is invited into the kitchen and fights with the cooks like Little John in the *Geste*! He is also pardoned by the king (at least in the story), and dies in a struggle with his enemies, killing his last adversary with his final blow.

Fulk Fitzwarin (the third) was among the barons who forced King John to accept Magna Carta in 1215, but his career as an outlaw began – and ended – much earlier. When his father died in 1197 he inherited a long-running legal battle to oust a rival claimant, Meurig of Powys, from the manor of Whittington in Shropshire, and refused to accept King John's decision in Meurig's favour. He resorted to brigandage, defying the authorities both in the marches and in Wiltshire, and proved himself as daring as he was disaffected. The King sent a force of 100 knights against him on one occasion, but finally, in November 1203, they were reconciled, and Fulk was granted Whittington on payment of 200 marks. It was again taken from him during the Magna Carta rebellion and not restored until well into Henry III's reign; but he thereafter lived peacefully until his death at the great age of *c*.80 in 1258.

Very little is known of Fulk – indeed, not much more that is known of Hereward – and the story of his three years as an outlaw survives only in a prose romance, *Fouke le Fitz Waryn*, first found in a compilation dating from 1325–40. Much of the material it contains is legendary, but again, there are some close parallels between Fulk's exploits and Robin's deeds in the *Geste*. Both their right-hand men are called John (Fulk has two, his brother John and John de Rampaigne), and both Little John and brother

John waylay travellers who are relieved of their wealth after they have dined. Little John successfully conceals his identity from the sheriff, while John de Rampaigne disguises himself so that he is not recognised by *his* master's great enemy, Sir Moris. Fulk is wounded in the leg when fleeing from Sir Noris. just as Little John is shot in the knee as he escapes from the sheriff, and both outlaw bands find sanctuary with a friendly knight, Fulk's with Sir Lewis (Prince Llewelyn) and Robin's with Sir Richard at the Lee. Both Sir Moris and the sheriff complain to their kings, John and Edward, before being slain by the hero of the story, and both monarchs then decide to deal with the outlaws personally. They are both lured into their enemies' camps by the promise of good hunting before being reconciled with the men they have come to capture, Robin entering Edward's service and John returning Fulk's lands. Robin subsequently asks permission to visit the chapel dedicated to Mary Magdalene he has founded in Barnsdale, and Fulk founds a priory in honour of Our Lady (another Mary) 'near Alberbury, in a wood, on the River Severn'. Both men are brigands, but both observe the same strict moral code. Robin 'did poor men much good', as we have already noticed, and 'neither Fulk nor any of his did damage at any time to anyone, save the King and his knights'.[1]

Another outlaw who both supported and opposed King John and whose story grew with the telling was the Boulonnais sea-captain, Eustace. Although known as 'Eustace the Monk' he abandoned religion while still a young man to avenge the murder of his father, and spent several years in the service of the Count of Boulogne. A dispute with the Count cost him his position in about 1204, and after waging a guerrilla war against his former master (and being outlawed for his trouble), he established himself in the Channel Islands and transferred his allegiance to King John.

He became feared as a pirate, and was granted lands in Norfolk for his good service; but when, in 1212, John and the Count became allies, Eustace offered his sword to the King of France. He commanded the ships that brought the King's son, Prince Louis, to England when the French tried to take advantage of the disruption caused by John's rejection of Magna Carta, and was beheaded as a traitor after his vessel was overwhelmed in a naval battle with the English fleet off Sandwich in August 1217. It is some measure of his reputation that his compatriots fled when they learned of his capture, and that English chroniclers regarded it as an act of God.[2]

Eustace's career was embellished in a romance, *Wistasse Li Moine*, written sometime between 1223 and 1284. It credits him with magical powers allegedly learned from Mephistopheles, and some episodes are similar to stories told of Robin, Herward and Fulk. Eustace is a master of disguise, tricking the Count by pretending to be a pilgrim, a leper on crutches, a merchant, a charcoal burner (one of Fulk's aliases), and, unsurprisingly, a potter crying his wares. Usually, the Count suffers only loss and ridicule (Eustace spares him when he falls into his hands just as Robin releases the sheriff in the first part of the *Geste*), but there are also harsher elements reminiscent of the *Monk* and *Guy of Gisborne*. A page has his tongue cut out to prevent him from telling his story, and four sergeants lose their feet, a fifth being sent to their master to explain why they cannot come themselves! Eustace too, asks his 'guests' how much money they are carrying, and rewards those who give him a truthful answer. A merchant of Flanders who admits to having £40 is sent on his way with the Monk's blessing, but the Abbot of Jumièges is robbed when the four silver marks he says he has turn out to be thirty. The parallel between Robin's treatment of Sir Richard at the Lee and the monks of St Mary's who fall into his hands is all too clear.

The Scottish patriot William Wallace was active nearly a century after Fulk and Eustace, but stories told of him incorporate some of the same popular themes. Mel Gibson's film *Braveheart* has raised his profile and made him easily the best known outlaw after Robin, although he more closely resembles Hereward as a leader of national resistance to an alien tyranny. He may have been born about 1270, but was unnoticed by contemporaries until he slew the Sheriff of Lanark and began to attract followers in 1297. His ability to organize and direct his forces gained him his famous victory over the English at Stirling Bridge in July, and he became 'guardian' of Scotland, granting lands and making treaties on behalf of the deposed king. Success came at a price however, and when Edward I marched north in person in 1298 some jealous knights and nobles refused to accept Wallace as their commander or to fight with him. He was heavily defeated at Falkirk, and although he remained in arms for the next seven years was never able to recover his former authority. King Edward was determined to hunt him down – he was specifically excluded from all reconciliations – and he was finally betrayed and captured in 1305. Taken to London, he was condemned without being allowed to speak in his own defence, and his dismembered quarters were displayed at Newcastle, Berwick, Perth, and, predictably, Stirling, as a grim warning to others.

Wallace's renown grew as the struggle between England and Scotland intensified, but it was not until near the end of the fifteenth century that Blind Harry the minstrel gathered the tales told of him into a 'grete buke'. Many of these are fictional, of course. Like Robin, the hero is a fine archer who fights injustice from his lair in the forest, and there are even occasions when he disguises himself as a monk and a potter. It would be tempting to bracket all these men together on the basis that their exploits drew on a common fund of traditional outlaw stories, but there is one crucial difference. Wallace, Hereward, Fulk and Eustace were men of substance, feudal tenants, who fought with and against kings: Robin is a more apolitical figure who has no ambitions to overthrow governments or reverse conquests. He is a hero *of* the people, not an aristocrat opposed to a tyrannical government who the people might suppose was on their side.

This can be seen most clearly in Robin's attitude towards the institutions of his day, the King, the Church, and the law. Medieval society, with its rich aristocrats and downtrodden peasants, was no egalitarian utopia; but Robin and those loyal to him never complained that bondmen who were obliged to till their lord's land for three days a week were being unfairly treated, and there is no record of them welcoming runaway villains or seeking to punish unjust stewards. They did not think that the lowest in society were being exploited, rather that the common good required each class to discharge its responsibilities to the others. God had allowed some men to enjoy greater privileges, and Robin always behaved respectfully towards those on a higher social level so long as they behaved properly towards him. His enemies – the sheriff and the Abbot of St Mary's – were particular individuals who were guilty of oppression, not men who had simply become too powerful or too rich.

It is not, of course, easy to be subject to a system while also appearing to be the arbiter of it, and Robin's stance leads him into some curious situations. The Robin of the ballads is an upholder of good law and an opponent of bad, or arbitrary legislation:

but who was to say which laws were 'good' and which 'bad'? A particular law might not be unreasonable *per se*, but could become oppressive if those charged with administering it were corrupt or lazy. Justice could – and sometimes did – become a mockery, and Robin felt entitled to use illegal violence to impose his own brand of fairness on those who were failing in their duty. In the ballads the king always sees the validity of the outlaws' rationale and forgives them, but in Robin's case the pardon is curiously ambivalent. He accepts forgiveness and agrees to enter King Edward's service, but on his own terms:

> But me lyke well your servyse,
> I wyll come agayne full soone,
> And shote at the donne [brown] dere
> As I am wonte to done.

No outlaw, as Professor Pollard points out, ever dictated the conditions of his own pardon, and although Robin recognizes royal authority, he 'challenges it, negotiates with it, and in the end defies it' when he returns to the forest without permission. The greenwood is an alternative kingdom with its own concept of 'popular' law.[3]

It is also clear that Robin is in many ways a composite character who effortlessly combines 'popular' activities such as archery, the giving of buffets, and poaching with the 'gentle' qualities of good manners, generosity and hospitality. When the outlaws are not using the bow they are swordsmen – the staff occurs only in *Robin Hood and the Potter*, and then it is the potter who wields it, not Robin. Similarly, the men who kill children and trick people when it suits them are the same as those who, on other occasions, claim to be high-minded and offer protection against oppression. Maurice Keen has commented that 'it is hard to reconcile the violent tone of [some] passages with the gay levity of others', while Professor Pollard remarks that the stories 'transform a gang of hardened highwaymen... into jocular, heroic, swashbuckling adventurers'. Stephen Knight is still more direct. The *Geste,* he notes, 'advocates massive theft from the church, civic insurrection against and murder of a properly appointed sheriff, breach of legitimate agreement with a king; and it imagines that all these things can lead to a lengthy and happy life... '.[4]

It is usually supposed that these apparent contradictions can be explained only in terms of audience satisfaction. Medieval minstrels would have entertained peasants as often as lords, and the stories they told had to appeal to all social classes. It is surely no coincidence that a 'good' knight who overcomes all adversity is one of the principal characters of the *Geste,* or that churchmen (who often railed against entertainers), are nearly always a 'bad lot'. But this is not to say that people were simply told what they wanted to hear: on the contrary, few would have paid, or rewarded, players whose tales were wholly unbelievable. Some modern commentators have emphasized Robin's supposedly humble yeoman status, but the term was one of several (armiger, scutifer, esquire), used interchangeably to describe the broad mass of lesser landowners until some time after 1300.[5] A real squire or gentleman could stand behind the Robin Hood legend just as the careers of Hereward, Fulk, Eustace and Wallace gave rise to the stories told of them.

It is clearly impractical to regard the ballads as even a semi-fictionalized biography of Robin and his followers,[6] but this does not mean that we cannot search them for clues to their historicity and which century of the later Middle Ages they seem to represent. The earliest stories associate Robin primarily with 'Barnsdale', a name that in the sixteenth century was applied to a wooded area of about five square miles north-west of Doncaster and south of Ferrybridge. It was never a royal forest, but was notorious as a haunt of brigands. In 1306, three Scottish churchmen, the bishops of St Andrews and Glasgow and the Abbot of Scone, who were being brought south as prisoners, had their escort doubled when they reached Barnsdale because the authorities feared they might be sprung or captured. Nearby are Wentbridge (which features in *Robin Hood and the Potter*), an important stopping-place for travellers on the Great North Road, and Sayles, where Little John and the others first encounter Sir Richard at the Lee in the *Geste*. Sayles was a small tenancy, a tenth of a knight's fee, in the manor of Pontefract, and only an author with detailed, local knowledge would have mentioned it. Its value as a look-out position over the Road is apparent, even today.[7]

Robin's main enemy in the stories ought to be the Sheriff of Yorkshire, but it is always the Sheriff of Nottingham. The earliest ballads usually begin in Barnsdale, but Nottingham, and its sheriff, always feature in them. Both of the *Geste's* archery contests are held there, it is where Robin sells his pots in the *Potter*, and where he is betrayed and captured in the *Monk*. It is the Sheriff of Nottingham who is first humiliated and then killed in the *Geste*, who is made to appear foolish in both the *Monk* and the *Potter*, and who dies again in *Robin Hood and Guy of Gisborne*. Sherwood forest is only mentioned occasionally, but there can be little doubt that when the outlaws escape after the archery contest, or when Robin (disguised as the potter) and the sheriff ride into the woods from Nottingham, they are entering Sherwood, not Barnsdale.

The royal forest of Sherwood extended to over 100,000 acres in the twelfth century, from Nottingham in the south to the river Meden in the north, and completely dwarfed its little northern neighbour. It became smaller in the thirteenth and fourteenth centuries as new developments encroached upon it, but was still favoured by the kings of that era. The three Edwards hunted in it on some twenty occasions in total, and Edward I is said to have held parliament there in 1290. It is possible that there were originally two cycles of ballads – one about Robin and Barnsdale and the other about the sheriff and Nottingham – and that these have become fused together: but equally, there seems no reason why Robin could not have ranged over both areas. The northern tip of Sherwood is only thirty miles from Barnsdale, and there were a number of occasions when kings, as well as outlaws, moved between them. In 1194, for example, Richard I chased a deer from Sherwood to Barnsdale, and nineteen years later King John travelled from Rothwell (just north of Barnsdale), to Nottingham in the space of a day. It has been suggested that the Barnsdale of the ballads is really Bryunsdale, near Basford on the edge of Nottingham, and Stephen Knight has proposed Barnsdale Forest in Rutland, twenty-five miles to the south-west. There are, he says, 'strong local traditions of outlaw activity in Tunneley Wood to the north', the names 'Robin Hood's field' and 'Robin Hood's cave' occur in the vicinity, and the Great North Road is only three miles away. Sir John Paston's remark that his servant had 'goon into Bernysdale' would also make more sense in this context (the Rutland Barnsdale lies between Norwich and Nottingham), but the references to Wentbridge, Sayles and other places seem to fix the location firmly in the north.[8]

The precise relationship between Barnsdale and Nottingham in the stories has long vexed modern writers on the subject, but medieval commentators do not seem to have been particularly concerned by it. There is little difference between the fragment of early fifteenth-century verse noticed in chapter one ('Robyn hod in scherewod stod, hodud [hooded] and hathud [hatted] and hosut [hosed] and schod'), and a curious legal formula, 'Robin Hode in Barnsdale stode', that first appears in a lawsuit in the court of Common Pleas in 1429.[9] A distinction can be made, however, between the apparent origins of the Sherwood and Barnsdale stories. Professor Holt has pointed out that, in general, those parts of the legend that derive from tales told of Hereward, Fulk and other outlaws relate to Nottingham, but it is more difficult to find analogues, or parallels, with those centred on Barnsdale and South Yorkshire. Themes like the hero disguising himself as a potter (in Nottingham in Robin's case), luring the sheriff into the forest, and ultimately recovering royal favour, were clearly popular literary motifs; but the stories of Robin's dealings with the poor knight who owes money to St Mary's Abbey, and the manner of his death at Kirklees, do not seem to occur elsewhere.[10] No townships, monasteries or roads in Sherwood are mentioned, and the area is as unreal as 'the "wood near Athens" of *A Midsummer Night's Dream*'. It appears that 'the nearer Robin gets to Nottingham the less authentic he becomes'.[11]

The real Robin is variously said to have lived between the end of the twelfth century and the first quarter of the fourteenth (between the reigns of Richard the Lionheart and Edward II), so do the ballads reflect a particular time or era? A number of references – or occasionally the lack of one – have been held to tie them to this or that period, but historians have sometimes interpreted the clues differently. It is true that in 1306 Edward I reduced the area of forest over which the Crown claimed jurisdiction by surrendering disputed districts to local communities, but this does not mean that those who lived within or near a royal forest were always 'happier' (and less inclined to bestow hero status on those who poached the vert and venison), thereafter. On the contrary, the harsh laws continued to be applied to the many places the King had not abandoned, and were still resented in 1381. It is true that there were no general visitations of Sherwood by the forest justices after 1286 until they went there for the last time in 1334; but Dr Maddicott has pointed out that these sessions still produced 'an impressive list of fines'.[12] The forest may not have been quite such a leading issue in the fourteenth century, but the problem had not gone away.

Similar arguments also apply to archery, which is a common feature of the earliest stories and particularly of the *Geste*. Their emphasis on the bow is sometimes thought to point to a later, rather than an earlier, date, because the weapon only acquired notoriety at Crecy (1346) and Agincourt (1415); but it would be a mistake to suppose that it was hardly used 100 years earlier. The men of Gwent were noted archers in the twelfth century, bowmen from the Kentish weald played a prominent part in the civil wars of 1216–17 and 1264–5, and Gerald of Wales, writing in 1188, tells of arrows that penetrated an oak door 'almost as thick as a man's palm', and of how one passed through a man's thigh and saddle before killing his horse.[13] Archery may have come into its own in the fourteenth century, but ordinary people had owned and used bows since before 1066.

Then there is Sir Richard at the Lee who the Robin of the *Geste* supposes has been 'made a knyght of force'. This is a clear reference to the practice of distraining (i.e. compelling) all those who had sufficient wealth to undertake the obligations of knighthood, but can it be related to a particular period? It was at its commonest in the reigns of Henry III and Edward I (1216–1307), but an outlaw who lived a little later would still have been familiar with it. Similarly, it has been argued that it would have been difficult for a knight to mortgage his lands to an abbot after the Statute of Mortmain forbade the alienation of feudal estates to the Church in 1279.[14] It was still possible however – anyone who wanted to make a donation to a religious body or raise funds from it could seek the Crown's permission – and Professor Pollard has pointed out that St Mary's Abbey was granted an exceptional general licence to acquire property up to the value of £200 per annum in 1301.[15] Regrettably, the abbey's own records, which might have confirmed this or similar transactions, have all been lost; but the technical information given, that failure to repay would result in foreclosure, shows that the ballad is no fairy story. It was set firmly in the realities of the day.

After Robin and Sir Richard, the *Geste's* most prominent – and most unpopular – character is undoubtedly the sheriff. It has been argued that sheriffs were at their most powerful – and were therefore most resented – before Edward I's reign began in 1272, but any suggestion that they were thereafter regarded as rather benign figures seems wide of the mark. It is true that sheriffs were rarely given authority over royal forests after the middle of the thirteenth century, but they were still regularly denounced by juries 100 years later and by Jack Cade's rebels as late as 1451. The ballad writers' animus towards the Sheriff of Nottingham may be more – but is not exclusively – relevant to the earlier period, and no firmer conclusions can be drawn from their failure to mention justices of the peace. JPs did not become conspicuous until the fourteenth century, and their absence from the stories could point to a date before 1300. But they were never hate figures like the sheriffs, and may have been ignored because they did not, by and large, trouble the outlaws. Complaints against them were relatively few.[16]

This leaves us with two pieces of evidence, one suggesting an earlier date of composition, the other later. Edward I's decision to relinquish control over parts of the royal forests allowed lords and others to convert some areas into private parks, chases and warrens, but there is no mention of these in the earliest ballads. Court records of the early fourteenth century document a great many offences committed in and against them (the new lordly owners were no more willing to allow the peasants free access than the king had been), and the only logical conclusion is that the stories belong to the period before 1306 when the forests were still wholly under royal authority. On the other hand, there are a number of references to the practice of retaining which became more common in the fourteenth century as the old feudal ties loosened. Relationships that had formerly been based on one man holding land of another were replaced by contracts under which those who agreed to serve received money fees and clothing (liveries); and it may be significant that in the *Geste* the justice has been bought by the abbot 'with cloth and fee', and the sheriff has to seek Sir Richard's permission to engage the disguised Little John for twenty marks (£13 6s 8d). John promises the sheriff's cook an annual fee of twenty marks and two new sets of clothes to induce him to join Robin's band, and John and Much receive £20 when they become yeomen of the Crown in *Robin Hood and the Monk*. There is one contrary example in *Robin Hood and Guy of Gisborne* when the sheriff tells the disguised Robin (who he believes to be Guy), that he could have had an old-fashioned feudal knight's fee for killing the outlaw, but the majority of these allusions are to the 'bastard' feudalism of a later date.

So, is it possible to draw any firm conclusions from this mass of apparently contradictory evidence? The answer is surely that the ballads changed with their audience. Change was inevitable as entertainers sang or talked their own versions of the tales over many generations, but more than this, they would have constantly, and instinctively, updated them. References to situations that had altered or were no longer current would have been more likely to puzzle the hearers than amuse them. The stories had to relate to a world they knew and understood, not one that had passed away a century or more earlier. Some of the original setting would be retained, of course, and would remain discernible no matter how much new material was heaped upon it; and this is why, paradoxically, it is possible to argue that the legend belongs to more than one period. Who is right then? Several commentators have argued for a fourteenth-century date on the grounds that if the stories had existed earlier they would have been mentioned in literature long before Langland wrote *Piers the Plowman* in about 1377; but we have seen that comments made by Langland and slightly later writers prove only that tales of Robin were then becoming increasingly popular. The logical conclusion is surely that the ballads originated in the thirteenth century, but acquired characteristics typical of the fourteenth as they were retold and developed. They became all things to all men.

3

THE ROBIN HOODS OF HISTORY

The Robin Hood ballads clearly drew on older traditions and grew with the telling, but surely there was a real outlaw whose deeds at least inspired the legend? A considerable number of Robins are mentioned in legal and administrative documents of the thirteenth and fourteenth centuries, and one or two of them are tolerably plausible candidates: but if they were notorious or famous why did contemporary historians completely ignore them?[1] The answer is that they were mostly petty criminals who had nothing to do with the later stories; but a great deal of ink has been spilt over some of them, and their 'claims' must be considered before they can be dismissed.

The earliest Robin we can trace in the records is a Robert Hood who was a servant of Alexander Nequam, Abbot of Cirencester, and who slew a man called Ralph of Cirencester in the abbot's garden at some time between 1213 and 1216. He was therefore a criminal of sorts, but there is no indication that he was outlawed or had any connection with Barnsdale and Sherwood. The same is true of a Robin 'Hod' who lived at Burntoft, in County Durham, and who gave surety to his neighbour, William Claxton, in 1244. His property, which the Claxtons subsequently acquired, was leased by them as 'Hodesplace' in the mid-fifteenth century, but we cannot even be certain that he fell foul of the law.[2]

A rather better candidate is a Robert of Wetherby 'outlaw and evildoer of our land' who the Sheriff of Yorkshire was ordered to capture and execute in July 1225. The pipe rolls (the annual accounts of the medieval Exchequer), record that the sheriff subsequently owed thirty-two shillings and sixpence in respect of the forfeited chattels of Robertus Hode, fugitive, and a marginal note next to one entry indicates that the debt was due from the Liberty of St Peter's, York. He must, therefore, have been a tenant of the archbishopric, but the plea roll that might have contained details of the charges against him is unfortunately lost. It is impossible to prove that Robert of Wetherby, outlaw, and Robert Hood, fugitive, were one and the same person, but his association with Wetherby would not have prevented him from living and working in another part of the county. He was evidently notorious – the sheriff not only hired men to catch him but bought a chain to hang his remains in public – and one pipe roll entry refers to him as 'Hobbehod'. This could imply that not only did he try to hide his face when he engaged in criminal activities, but that he may also have ridden a 'hobby', a small horse.[3]

These references are few and scattered, but there is a distinct concentration of persons who bore the unusual name 'Robinhood' in the south-east of England in the latter half of the thirteenth century. A William Robehod was a member of a gang suspected of robberies and of harbouring robbers in Berkshire in 1261–2; and in 1272 a man named as John Rabunhod was outlawed after he and others were accused of killing one John, son of Simon, in a tavern brawl at Charford in Hampshire. In the same year an Alexander Robehod was sought for theft in Essex; pledges secured the release of one Gilbert Robehod after he had been charged with an unspecified offence in Suffolk in 1286; and a Robert Robehod was accused of stealing sheep in Hampshire in 1294.

It would be easy to suppose that these men, who just happened to be called Robinhood, also just happened to be petty criminals, but there is good evidence that this was not the case. The Berkshire gang-member noticed above is called William Robehod on the memoranda roll of the King's Remembrancer in the Exchequer for Easter 1262, but the corresponding entry on the plea roll of the Justices in Eyre (travelling justices, who in theory visited each county annually) gives his name as William, son of Robert le Fevere (i.e. Smith). There can be virtually no doubt that William Robehod and William 'Smith' were one and the same person since the Justices' statement that William le Fevere's chattels, valued at 2s 6d, had been seized by the prior of Sandleford without warrant, can be matched with the Remembrancer's clerk's note that the King had pardoned the penalty of one mark imposed on the prior for taking William Robehod's possessions without authority. What had happened was that someone along the administrative chain between the Justices and the Remembrancer had changed 'Smith' to 'Robehod', a nickname his activities clearly merited. It would be tempting to go one step further and say that the person who made the amendment must have known the stories of Robin the famous outlaw; but he may only have been alluding to robbers generally and to their tendency to wear hoods.

Unsurprisingly, what had hitherto been a nickname for bandits soon became a recognized surname. There is nothing to suggest that two other Robinhoods who appear in Huntingdonshire in 1285 and 1296 were miscreants, nor was Gilbert Robynhod of Fletching in Sussex (not the Gilbert mentioned above, apparently), who paid his taxes in 1296. The same is true of a Katherine Robynhod who was living in London in 1325, and a Robert Robynhoud recorded at West Harting in Sussex seven years later. Katherine was probably a daughter of the Robin Hood who was a common councillor of London at the beginning of the fourteenth century, and who gave his name to an inn, the *hostel Robin Hod*, in Vintry Ward in the City. He seems to have been a highly respected individual, far removed from the disreputable ancestor whose activities (we may surmise) had once tarnished the family. Katherine's surname was clearly a patronymic, and implied no wrongdoing on her part.[4]

Still more Robins have been found in the court rolls of the manor of Wakefield, ten miles from Barnsdale. There was Robert Hode of Newton near Alverthorpe who appeared at various sessions of the manor court between 1308 and 1329; two Robert Hoddes of Sowerby who are mentioned from 1313 onwards; a Robert Hood the Grave[5] who was penalized in 1309 for breaking the lord of the manor's fold at Alverthorpe (and who might, therefore, have been Robert of Newton); and, most interestingly, a Robert Hode of Wakefield, who features in the sequence of rolls that ends in 1317 but who does not reappear when they again become available after 1323. This Robert seems to have been a man of some substance since he employed at least one maidservant and leased several small parcels of land in nearby townships. He was fined several times for minor offences (taking wood, etc.), and on one occasion was involved in fighting with, or chastising, two women. In 1316 he and his wife Matilda paid two shillings with an annual rent of eighteen pence for a plot of their lord's land on Bichill (Bitchill, Bickhill, the market place of Wakefield), and he was included in a list of those who failed to attend a muster for military service in November. This is the last direct reference to him, but in October

1357 William Hallstede and his wife surrendered a tenement on Bichill that had once been held by Robert Hode.[6]

The first person to suggest that Robert Hode of Wakefield could have been the Robin of legend was Joseph Hunter, a Yorkshireman who began his career as a Presbyterian minister, and who was appointed an assistant keeper of the new Public Record Office (now the National Archives), in 1838. This gave him an unrivalled opportunity to look for evidence that would confirm the stories of Robin the Outlaw in the ballads, and he established that Edward II's progress through Yorkshire and Lancashire between August and November 1323 mirrored the itinerary of 'Edward, our comely king' in the *Geste*. Edward was at Nottingham between 9 and 23 November, and it was near Nottingham that the King supposedly pardoned Robin and took him into his service. Hunter then turned to the records of the royal household and, remarkably, discovered a Robyn Hode who was employed as a porter of the Chamber between March and October 1324. The ballad Robin feigned sleeplessness and loss of appetite to persuade the King to allow him to return to the greenwood, and interestingly, Robyn the porter was given five shillings when his employment ended 'because he can no longer work'.

Hunter's theory was that Robert Hode of Wakefield had supported Earl Thomas of Lancaster's uprising against Edward II, and became a forest outlaw after the rebels were defeated at Boroughbridge in 1322. It attracted little notice at the time, but was taken up by another Yorkshireman, J.W. Walker, in an article written in 1944 and a book published in 1952.[7] Walker found five 'stalls' newly erected on Bichill among properties apparently forfeited by the rebels, converted them into a dwelling house 'of five chambers', and suggested that they should be identified with the tenement acquired by Robert and Matilda Hode six years earlier. He believed that because Robert had been summoned to join the army mustered for service in Scotland in 1316, he would certainly have been required to assist Earl Thomas at Boroughbridge, and proved to his own satisfaction that Robyn the porter was not mentioned in the Household wardrobe books before 1323. In his opinion they were one and the same.

Unfortunately, it is not quite that simple. The muster rolls that would have resolved the question of precisely who joined the rebels are no longer extant, but it may be significant that Robert had been fined three pence for *failing* to serve in 1316, and might not, therefore, have been summoned subsequently. He was not among the sixty or so tenants named on the contrariants' roll for Wakefield (an account of lands, rents and goods forfeited by the rebels compiled by one Thomas Deyvill), and Sir James Holt has shown that the five 'stalls' mentioned had not been seized from a contrariant but were part of the usual revenues of the town.[8] Walker did not consider the possibility that Robert of Wakefield could have died soon after 1317, or escaped mention in the rolls after 1323. He also failed to appreciate that the porters were not always named individually, and that Robyn the porter could have been present in the Household even if he did not appear in the accounts.

But do Hunter's discoveries relating to King Edward's itinerary and Robyn the porter confirm that some of the incidents described in the ballads really happened? There is nothing to prove that Robert Hode of Wakefield was the Robyn Hode of the King's chamber, and no evidence that Robert was ever associated with Thomas of Lancaster or committed more than very minor offences. Professor Bellamy has pointed to a number of discrepancies between the known dates of the King's progress and the sequence of events described in the *Geste*,[9] but the fact remains that the ruler who forgave the ballad Robin was called Edward, and that one of his prime concerns was the slaying of the deer in the royal forests. A recently discovered fragment of a day-book of the chamber which shows that Robyn the porter *was* in the King's employ as early as June 1323 (and could not, therefore, have been pardoned at Nottingham in November), has been held to discredit Hunter's theory; but Edward visited the city on more than one occasion in 1323 and could have met Robin when he was there in March or perhaps April. Again, we do not know if he was being paid before this – the information is simply not available – but the period from June 1323 to November 1324 is not incompatible with the 'twelve months and three' he is said to have been in royal service in the *Geste*. The ballad writers were telling a story in which precise dates were unimportant, and they may have had only a very general recollection of events of the past.

All this sounds quite persuasive, but is it true? Is it likely that Edward II would have pardoned a man who had fought against him and poached his deer, and would he have taken him into his service? He could have done, but other rebels were treated far less generously. Thomas of Lancaster was beheaded after the merest semblance of a trial (without being allowed to speak in his own defence), and at least twenty-seven other leading contrariants were executed, many of them after being taken back to their own localities where their rotting corpses would serve as a dire warning to their friends and tenants. The chroniclers estimate that somewhere between sixty-two and a hundred others were imprisoned, a fate shared by some of their wives and children including Earl Thomas's wife, Alice de Lacy, and her elderly mother the Countess of Lincoln. More than 1,000 other lesser individuals suspected of being involved with their lords in the uprising were arrested, and many were fined or lost their holdings. Interestingly, the heaviest penalties were imposed on a group of Earl Thomas's Yorkshire retainers, clear evidence that the King was no better disposed towards rebels from that county than from others. Some who were related to men who had remained loyal were able to obtain partial amelioration of their punishment, but the majority were treated harshly. If Robin really was involved in the rebellion, he would have needed to be a man of almost unimaginable charm and charisma to win the goodwill of a vengeful Edward II.

So does this mean that the story told in the *Geste* is wholly imaginary? Well, not entirely, because the conditions created by the royal ruthlessness were those in which outlaws could and did flourish. There was widespread plundering of the contrariants' properties, and the King refused to honour Earl Thomas's debts or to automatically reinstate the leases of the estates seized from him.[10] Sheriffs and mayors were ordered to seek out lesser individuals who had supported the uprising, and this, as Natalie Fryde points out, must have given some of them ample opportunity to indict unpopular members of the community while protecting those nearest to them. Men who had lost everything, and who had no one to plead for them, turned to brigandage, and lived by their wits until they were captured. There was John Wyard, who in 1324 was raiding and looting in Worcestershire, while a force of twenty-four men-at-arms and 400 footmen led by John Mowbray, Jocelyn d'Eyvill and Hugh Eland plundered villages in the Honour of Tickhill (Yorkshire) as late as 1326. These men were not Robin Hoods, still less Robin the Outlaw, but it is easy to see how some of their activities could have stoked the legend and contributed to it. King Edward was certainly in the right area in 1323, but it is more likely that he would have hung the outlaw Robin than given him a job!

There are other real Robin Hoods, for example, a Robert Hode who lived at Howden (Yorkshire) in Edward II's reign but about whom we know almost nothing, a namesake imprisoned for no less a crime than trespass of vert and venison in Rockingham forest in Northamptonshire in 1354, and a third, otherwise known as Robert Dore of Wadsley (Yorkshire), who was outlawed for his involvement in the Poll Tax riots before being pardoned in May 1382. This last Robert is of some interest because the Dores held land in Loxley near Robin's alleged birthplace, but the 'connection' seems to be no more than a coincidence.[11] Indeed, it is apparent that although all the individuals considered bore the same name, lived at approximately the right time, and in some cases got into trouble, none of them did anything that would have fired the popular imagination and made them into national heroes. We will have to seek the real Robin elsewhere.

The first references to an historical – as opposed to a literary – Robin are found in the writings of two Scottish chroniclers of the fifteenth century, Andrew of Wyntoun, who was Prior of St Serf's Inch in Loch Leven, and the Abbot of Incholm, Walter Bower. Andrew of Wyntoun, was an old man with a long memory when he composed his *Metrical Chronicle* about 1420, and has this under the year 1283:

Than litill Jhone and Robyne Hude
Waichmen [highwaymen] were commendit gud, [well-renowned]
In Yngilwode and Bernysdale
And usit this tyme thar travale.
[And all this time they plied their trade]

Walter Bower, who wrote a continuation of Fordun's *Scotishronicon* in the 1440s, thought that they were disinherited supporters of Simon de Montfort, forced into outlawry after the Earl's defeat and death at the battle of Evesham in 1265:

> Then arose the famous murderer, Robert Hood, as well as Little John, together with their accomplices from among the dispossessed, whom the foolish populace are so inordinately fond of celebrating both in tragedy and comedy.[12]

We cannot tell what information Wyntoun and Bower had before them – it may have been no more than the ballads – and the former's reference to Inglewood suggests some confusion between Robin and Adam Bell and his friends (see Appendix 1). But they both thought that Robin was a real person, and their dates for him are only seventeen years apart. The real puzzle of course, is why no contemporary *English* chronicler says something similar. Robin should, logically, feature more strongly in their narratives than in the works of two obscure Scots, but they tell us nothing. One reason may be that English monastic writers were reluctant to celebrate the life of a man who, if the ballads are accurate, tricked the king, lampooned those in authority, and robbed and even killed clergymen. Walter Bower had little regard for him, but at least he served as an example of what awful things could and did happen in England![13]

Remarkably, only a few weeks after these words were written, a new discovery by Dr Julian Luxford was reported in the newspapers. Headed '23 words that debunk legend of Robin Hood' in the *Daily Mail*, and, more comprehensively, 'History is debunked' in *The Independent on Sunday*, it referred to a marginal note in a copy of Ranulf Higden's *Polychronicon* which (the reports claimed), proved that Robin was not universally popular and did not 'rob the rich to give to the poor'. Written by a monk at Witham Abbey in Somerset, perhaps about 1460, the note says that 'around this time, according to popular opinion, a certain outlaw named Robin Hood, with his accomplices, infested Sherwood and other law-abiding areas of England with continuous robberies'. It does not state precisely when Robin lived, but has been added to a folio which begins with an account of Edward I's second Welsh war and the accession of Pope Boniface VIII in 1294, and ends with the King's marriage to Margaret of France in 1299. The English destruction of forests used by the Welsh as hiding places and William Wallace's revolt are also mentioned, but, as Dr Luxford points out, there is nothing to suggest that either of these facts persuaded the annotator to insert his comment at this point in the manuscript. His work 'demonstrates a scrupulous concern for historical and chronological accuracy', and he presumably had access to a source which placed Robin's activities in these years.[14]

Any comparatively early reference to Robin is bound to be of interest, but does it tell us anything new? The idea that he was a popular philanthropist is only mentioned obliquely in the *Geste* (see chapter 1), and there is no certainty that the legend the monk was allegedly 'debunking' even existed when he added his comment. If he had heard, or read, some of the earliest stories of Robin he would have known that monks were among his principal enemies, and would have been only too aware that outlaws in general threatened the wealthier sections of society. His remark is perhaps no more – or less – than we would expect from a man in his position who derived his information from what he himself termed 'popular opinion', but was popular opinion really so biased? Within a decade, two men who fomented risings designed to support Warwick the Kingmaker's attempts to recover influence with Edward IV used the pseudonyms 'Robin of Redesdale' and 'Robin of Holderness' to disguise their identities. The 'Robin' they were alluding to was almost certainly Robin Hood, and they did not, apparently, think that invoking his memory would discourage people from joining them. Robin may have been unpopular with rich, idle clerics, but it would be a mistake to assume that our monk spoke for all.

The monk probably knew much less about Robin than we do, but he seems to have been in no doubt that he was talking about a real person. His comment, although slightly later than the references in Wyntoun's and Bower's chronicles, would still make him the first *English* writer to assume that here was something that was more than a fable and worth mentioning. We should not make too many assumptions, of course. A comment written in a distant West Country monastery some 200 years after the event can hardly be considered prime evidence, and can only reflect the opinions – and prejudices – of one man at one moment in time. But it is interesting, nevertheless.

4

FRIENDS, FOES & GRAVESTONES

The Robin Hood ballads were not, as we have noted, written for the benefit of future historians, and there are many occasions when they are infuriatingly – if understandably – imprecise. We have already seen that Robin Hood could itself be a pseudonym, and 'Little John' must fall into the same category. The Sheriff of Nottingham is known only by his title (we are never given a personal name that would allow us to identify him), and the same is true of other great office-holders like the Abbot of St Mary's, York. We appear to be on slightly firmer ground with Will Scarlett and Sir Richard at the Lee; but there seems to have been almost as many Wills as Robins, and no Sir Richard in the right place at the right time. So are they wholly imaginary, or are the stories told of them based on the careers of identifiable individuals who achieved at least some slight fame?

Little John, Robin's principal lieutenant, is perhaps the most important figure in the tales after Robin himself, but we do not learn much about him personally. In one place in the *Geste* he tells the sheriff that he is a native of Holderness in Yorkshire and that 'Men cal me Reynolde Grenelef whan I am at home', but there is no reason to suppose that he would have revealed his true

identity to an arch enemy. One tradition says that his surname was
Nailer and a John le Nailer is mentioned in the Wakefield Court
Rolls in 1329, but evidence that he was the John of the ballads is
entirely lacking.[1] The problem is that Little John – or John Little
– was almost as common a name as Robert Hood. Professor Holt
mentions a Little John and a Petit Johan who were both appealed
of robbery in 1292,[2] and Professor Bellamy has identified no fewer
than five possible candidates who lived in the early fourteenth
century. A John le Littel served Queen Isabella as a palfreyman
and sumpterman in 1311/12, and two others were among a group
of men who attacked the property of Simon de Wakefield at
Hornington (Yorkshire) in or shortly before December 1318, and
made off with £138. One of these, whose domicile is not recorded,
had a brother named Elias, and the other came from Leicester and
had a brother called Simon. Perhaps more significantly, Archbishop
Melton of York complained in 1323 that one John 'Littel John'
and other malefactors had killed deer in his park at Beverley, and
Edward II simultaneously employed a man with this name as a
sailor. The first references to him are in September and October
1322, and he was still in service when the King paid him 3s 6d to
sail from Porchester to the Isle of Wight in September 1324, and
five shillings to transport his goods from Nottingham to London
by sea in January 1325.[3]

Little John the mariner was based at Hull for a time, and
Professor Bellamy suggests he could also have been the John who
broke into Archbishop Melton's park at Beverley. Beverley is only
ten miles from Hull and is adjacent to Holderness where the John of
the *Geste* claimed he was born; but a conviction for poaching deer
in the area would not identify him as Robin Hood's companion.
Most medieval sailors had, as Bellamy recognizes, 'earned their

living on the sea from their youth', and it is most unlikely that John the forester would have become captain of a ship in middle life. It is, of course, interesting, that this John was serving the King at the same time that Robyn Hode was employed as a porter of the Chamber, but neither appears to have been a reformed outlaw! The name did not automatically imply wrongdoing (unlike the 'Robinhoods' noticed in the last chapter), and some who bore it were respected citizens. A slightly later John Litel was sheriff of London on several occasions between 1354 and 1367 and an alderman in 1374.

Of Robin's other companions, not much can be said about Much the Miller's son (pun intended!), except that mills were plentiful in Yorkshire in the Middle Ages. Both Much and Will Scarlett appear in the *Geste* and in *Robin Hood and the Monk*,[4] and Will also features in *Guy of Gisborne* and in the story of Robin's death. His name is variously rendered as Scarlok, Scarloke, Scatheloke, and Scathelocke in the *Geste*, *as* Scathlock in the *Monk*, and as Scarllett and Scarlett in *Guy* and in *Robin Hoode his Death*,[5] and Professor Bellamy has collected particulars of no fewer than six men who were so called and who were active between 1286 and 1347. Interestingly, one was a novice of St Mary's Abbey, York, who had left the institution under a cloud (in about 1286 or 87), while another was a long serving member of the Berwick garrison who in December 1316 was offered maintenance (his keep, as a form of pension), in Whitby Abbey. Two Will Scarletts were pardoned in November 1318 and October 1327, another was paid 28s 2d by the chamberlain of Scotland in April 1305, and a fourth was granted a rent of three shillings a year from a messuage in Braughing (Hertfordshire) in 1347. Some of these could, possibly, be identified with others, but none of them is obviously the Will of the ballads. The *Geste says* that of the 'seven score and thre' outlaws Robin promised would join him in royal service when the King pardoned him, only John and 'good Scathelocke' were still with him when he decided to return to the greenwood. We would expect to find them being paid alongside Robyn Hode the porter in Joseph Hunter's scenario, but the records are silent. An Adam Schakelok of Crigglestone appears in the Wakefield Court Rolls in April 1317, but there is no evidence that he had a relative called Will.

Another early member of the band, but one who has not caught the popular imagination in the same way that Little John and Will have, was Gilbert of the White Hand. His skill as an archer is mentioned in the *Geste* on two occasions, but he does not feature in the stories in any other context. His intriguing name is reminiscent of Robert Blanchemains, 'white-handed', the third Beaumont Earl of Leicester (1168–90), who is remembered chiefly for the devastation he brought on the town when he supported the rebellion of Henry II's sons against their father in 1173. There is nothing to suggest that either the legendary Gilbert or the real Robert were incapacitated – Earl Robert actually died on the Third Crusade – so their white hands were presumably not the result of scar tissue or poor circulation. A more likely explanation is the condition known as vitiligo, a disorder that causes loss of pigment resulting in irregular pale patches of skin. No one knows how, or why, this happens, but it is thought that genetic and environmental factors, or even stress, can combine to induce the immune system to inexplicably eliminate some natural colouring. Between one and two per cent of the population are affected, so it would not have been uncommon in the Middle Ages. Perhaps Earl Robert and the man the Gilbert character was based on suffered from it more severely – and obviously – than others.[6] P.V. Harris found the surname Withondes, Wythehoundes, and variants in the Wakefield Court Rolls, but no Gilbert who might be our man.

Little John and Will Scarlett were common names found in many everyday situations, but there is no record of a plausible Sir Richard at the Lee. The Wakefield Court Rolls mention a 'Richard of the Lee' who sued 'William of the Watirhouses' at Rastrick in April 1317,[7] and Professor Bellamy has argued the claims of a Richard de la Lee who was parson of Arksey, near Doncaster, from July 1319 until the first half of 1321.[8] This Richard was living within seven miles of Barnsdale in the period just before Thomas of Lancaster's rebellion; acknowledged debts of five marks, seven marks, and £11 10s at various times in 1321 and 1322; and was imprisoned in Colchester Castle for poaching venison in Waltham forest after being appointed to the parish of Bradwell, in Essex, in 1327. But a clerk does not sound much like the knight of the ballad, and the fact that his third debt was enrolled in chancery in May 1322 shows that he was not then an outlaw. Indeed, there is no evidence that he was ever outlawed at all.

The knight who has mortgaged his lands to St Mary's Abbey is not named in the first part of the *Geste* – he is only called Sir Richard when Robin and his men seek refuge in his castle near Nottingham – and this has led to suggestions that there are really two men of knightly status whose stories have been woven together in the ballad. The first returns home to 'Verysdale' after repaying his debt to the abbot, a place usually identified with Wyresdale, to the west of the forest of Bowland in Lancashire.[9] There is a hamlet called Lee where the road from Bowland to Lancaster crosses the Wyre, and it was his son's slaying of a 'knyght of Lancaster' that had caused his difficulties. Wyresdale is clearly not the 'fayre castell, A lytell within the wode; Double dyched it was about, And walled, by the rode' that protected the outlaws in what must have been Sherwood, but there is no reason why such a man should not have possessed two homes, or properties. Sir Richard is profuse in his thanks for the outlaws' past help when he gives them shelter, and the writer may have deliberately 'toned down' his first appearance to lessen his prominence in the tale.

The story of the knight is at once more sophisticated than many of the *Geste's* other motifs which involve tricks, disguises and sometimes gratuitous violence. The granting and repaying of loans is an altogether duller subject, but it is lightened by an emphasis on courtesy and polite behaviour which makes the Robin of the ballads a more attractive figure. The same is true of Maid Marian and Friar Tuck, who are both relatively late additions to the stories but who have become so popular that some mention must be made of them. There was, as we noticed in chapter one, a separate cycle of Marian ballads. A French pastoral play, *Robin et Marion*, written *c.*1283, tells of how Marian, a shepherdess, resists the advances of a knight to remain true to her lover Robin; but she was not connected with the English outlaw Robin until he became synonymous with the Robin of the May games between 1450 and 1500. Supporters of the Robert Hood of Wakefield who appears in the Court Rolls in the early 1300s note that he had a wife called Matilda, a name not too far removed from Marian. But this obscure lady does not seem a very likely prototype for a royal ward who risks everything to live with Robin in the woods.

Friar Tuck is rather different, because Robert Stafford, a chaplain in the parish of Linfield, in Sussex, assumed the name 'ffrere Tuke' when he led an outlaw band in the early fifteenth century. His inclusion in a surviving fragment of a play 'Robin Hood and the Sheriff', based on the earlier story of *Guy of Gisborne*, shows that he was associated with Robin by *c.*1475, but did Stafford invent the name or had an earlier renegade priest become a symbol of popular resistance to authority? There were no friars in England until 1221, so it would have been impossible for Robin to have met such a man in the reign of Richard the Lionheart. But a house of Grey Friars was founded at Broadmarsh, near Nottingham Castle, in 1250, and their numbers increased rapidly thereafter. Professor Holt notes that the men who drafted the writs against Stafford in 1417 were unfamiliar with his alias, so 'Tuck' was not then a traditional name for a clerical bandit.[10] It could refer to the way in which friars sometimes 'tucked' the skirts of their habits into their belts to make it easier to negotiate overgrown paths and muddy tracks, or perhaps Stafford the outlaw simply 'took' from his victims. He was not a friar himself, of course, but the mendicant orders were becoming notorious for their wealth and avarice, and for committing what people thought amounted to daylight robbery. Chaucer's friar was 'wanton' and 'mery', readily gave absolution for money, and 'though a widewe hadde but a shoo [shoe] Yet wold he have a farthing or [before] he went'.[11]

This is all we can say of Robin's friends – Alan, or Allen, a Dale, George a Green, the 'Jolly Pinder' of Wakefield,[12] and others do not seem to have joined his band until the sixteenth or seventeenth centuries – so what of his foes, most notably the Sheriff of Nottingham? The sheriff was the King's viceroy in the area assigned to him, and although his importance diminished from the thirteenth century onwards he remained responsible for collecting some royal revenues, overseeing the election of members of Parliament, holding inquests, arresting criminals, and summoning juries. Robin and his men would have been summoned to appear at four successive county courts to answer the charges against them, and if they failed to do so would have been outlawed and their goods confiscated. They would have felt only antipathy towards a man who, besides serving the writs on them (if he could find them) and assembling a posse to pursue and catch them, might choose jurors who he was sure would bring in verdicts against them. All the outlaws had to do, in theory, was to cross the border into a county in which they were not 'wanted', but both Nottinghamshire and Yorkshire seem to have been equally 'no-go' areas for Robin and his men.

The first problem we encounter in trying to identify a particular individual as Robin's sheriff is that, strictly speaking, there was no Sheriff of Nottingham at this time. The Sheriff and Chief Forester of Nottinghamshire and Derbyshire, the Constable of Nottingham Castle, and the Justice of the Forests beyond Trent all had responsibilities that could have brought them into conflict with the outlaws, and there is no shortage of possible candidates. In the early thirteenth century there is Philip Mark, who was Sheriff of Nottinghamshire and Derbyshire from 1209 to 1224 and custodian of Sherwood between 1212 and 1217; Brian de Lisle, who was Chief Forester of Nottinghamshire and Derbyshire 1209–17, Chief Justice of the Forest 1221–4, and Sheriff of Yorkshire in 1233–4; and Eustace of Lowdham (Nottinghamshire) who was Sheriff and then Deputy Sheriff of Yorkshire in 1225–6, a Forest Justice north of the Trent in 1226, and Sheriff of Nottinghamshire and Derbyshire in 1232–3. Eustace is particularly interesting because he was the Deputy Sheriff of Yorkshire responsible for selling the chattels of the mysterious Robertus Hode, fugitive, and accounting to the exchequer for the proceeds, in 1226.

Any of these three men could have been Robin Hood's enemy, but so too could four others who held office in the early fourteenth century. Sir Robert Ingram served as Sheriff of Nottinghamshire and Derbyshire in 1322–3, 1327–8 and again, briefly in 1334, and was Mayor of Nottingham on four occasions between 1315 and 1324. He was five times elected Member of Parliament for the town, and was returned as a knight of the shire for Nottinghamshire in 1325 and 1328 (twice), and for Derbyshire in 1334 and 1340 (twice). He must have been well known in the north Midlands, but his friendly relations with the notorious Coterel gang (see chapter 6) would not suggest that he was disliked by outlaws generally. John de Segrave was never a sheriff, but he served as keeper of Nottingham Castle between 1308 and 1325, and was an unpopular justice of the forests beyond Trent between 1308 and 1315. His activities could have brought him into conflict with a later Robin, but again, there is no evidence that this was the case.

Ingram was succeeded as Sheriff of Nottinghamshire and Derbyshire in June 1323 by Sir Henry de Faucumberg who also briefly replaced John de Segrave as keeper of Nottingham Castle on the latter's death in 1325. Faucumberg was an 'old hand' who had already been pricked as Sheriff of Nottinghamshire and Derbyshire in 1318–19, and who served as Sheriff of Yorkshire for nearly five years in total between April 1325 and December 1330. It was during his second period of office in Nottinghamshire and Derbyshire that Edward II visited Nottingham in November 1323 (in the aftermath of Earl Thomas of Lancaster's rebellion), and appointed a commission of oyer and terminer to examine various malpractices which had allegedly occurred in the area. One of those accused – of being responsible for false indictments and imprisonments, extorting and embezzling money, and practising 'unjust and intolerable restraints' – was none other than his own sheriff Faucumberg, who also features in a list of local officials suspected of corruption drawn up in the summer of 1326. These misdemeanours would not have endeared him to an early fourteenth-century outlaw, and it may also be significant that the name Henry Faucumberg appears no fewer than five times in the Wakefield manor court rolls between 1313 and 1328. Professor Bellamy identifies this individual with Faucumberg the sheriff (the name is most unusual), but again, there is nothing to suggest that he had dealings with any of the Wakefield Robins. And the possibility of one of them being Robin the Outlaw seems slight.[13]

A rather later sheriff who has attracted considerable attention is John de Oxenford, who served in Nottinghamshire and Derbyshire for more than four years between 1334 and 1339. Oxenford was a man of limited means who failed to achieve knighthood (the usual qualification for a sheriff's office), but he was no less venal than his predecessors. The outbreak of the Hundred Years' War in 1336 placed new demands on men at all levels of society, and a commission appointed to investigate complaints heard that he had taken corn from forty-three villages without payment (for his own use rather than the King's according to his critics), and had seized over 200 oxen and 12,000 sheep, later selling them back to their owners for his own profit. Anyone with a clear conscience would have wanted to refute these and other allegations that he had taken bribes and used his position as sheriff to extort money, but Oxenford simply failed to appear. He was accordingly outlawed in July 1341 (a 'nice irony' remarks Dr Maddicott), and, although pardoned, was never restored to office. He was notorious enough to be the sheriff of the ballads, and may have passed through Barnsdale when he went to present his accounts to the Exchequer at York; but again, there is nothing to connect him with Robin or with particular incidents described in the tales.[14]

Oxenford's candidacy would, arguably, be enhanced if it could be shown that a grasping Abbot of St Mary's, York, and a corrupt justice were active at the same period, and Dr Maddicott has proposed Thomas de Multon, abbot from 1332 to 1359, and Geoffrey le Scrope, Chief Justice of the King's Bench between 1324 and 1338. St Mary's was wealthy and well able to lend large sums of money (Edward I borrowed £4,000 in 1304, for example), and the Close Rolls record that Multon advanced sums to no fewer than sixteen individuals or groups of persons while the chancery was based in York between October 1332 and February 1336. We do not, unfortunately, know how hard he pressed his creditors, but an incident in 1336 – when he used threats to replace a vicar with his own candidate – shows that he was not above resorting to doubtful methods on occasion. The Court of King's Bench also operated from York for much of the 1330s (Edward III's Scottish wars brought many of the functions of government northwards), and Justice Scrope would have had many opportunities to become familiar with Abbot Multon. There is evidence that he, too, was prepared to bend the rules when it suited him, but so were many other abbots and justices of the period. They happened to be in the same place for part of the same decade, but there is no record of any direct, formal relationship between them and they were not singled out for particular criticism. They could have come into contact with Oxenford, but there is nothing to connect them with a Sir Richard at the Lee or a Robin Hood.

Still more opaque (from our viewpoint), are the Prioress of Kirklees and her lover Sir Roger of Doncaster. Joseph Hunter pointed to an Elizabeth de Staynton, whose family held land near to Barnsdale, and who was a nun at Kirklees in 1344. The *Geste* says that Robin died twenty-two years after he left the king's service, so Elizabeth could have been the prioress who betrayed the former porter of the Chamber – if the former porter of the Chamber was betrayed by anyone – in about 1346 or 1347. Unfortunately however, there is no evidence that Elizabeth ever rose to become prioress of Kirklees or was related to a family of Hoods, and no knight called Roger of Doncaster has been discovered in either the late thirteenth or early fourteenth centuries although the name was far from uncommon. Professor Bellamy has pressed the claims of a priest, 'sir Roger de Doncastria', who was active between at 1302 and 1333. This Roger was vicar of Ruddington, in Nottinghamshire, and at the latter date was awaiting trial for trespass of vert in Sherwood; but he does not seem to have been connected with Kirklees, and more evidence is needed before we can say that he 'was the abettor of the prioress in her murderous plot'.[15]

It is unlikely that genuine, tangible reminders of these people will still exist after such a long period, but Robin, Little John, and Will Scarlett all have marked graves. According to one ballad version, the dying Robin shot an arrow to indicate where he wanted to be buried, but the Tudor writer Richard Grafton thought that the Prioress of Kirklees had interred him beside the road:

> where he had used to rob and spoyle those that passed that way. And upon his grave the sayde prioresse did lay a very fayre stone, wherein the names of Robert Hood, William of Goldesborough, and others were graven. And the cause why she buryed him there was, for that the common strangers and travailers, knowyng and seeyng him there buryed, might more safely and without feare take

their jorneys that way, which they durst not do in the life of the sayd outlawes. And at either end of the sayde tombe was erected a crosse of stone, which is to be seen there at this present[16]

A drawing made by the Pontefract antiquarian Nathaniel Johnston in 1665 shows a slab decorated with a cross 'fleuree' (the standing crosses had presumably disappeared by his day), and the inscription 'Here lie Roberd Hude, Willm Goldburgh, Thoms... ' carved round the edge. Nothing is known of William of Goldesborough or Thomas (unless the former was an alternative name for Will Scarlett), and the inscription was said to be 'scarce legible' some years before Johnston drew it. Robin could have been buried in a grave that already contained other bodies, but if the monument was erected shortly after his death (whenever *that* was), it is curious that there is no mention of it before about 1540. The priory came into the possession of the Armitage family after the Dissolution of the monasteries, and in the early eighteenth century Sir Samuel Armitage had the ground beneath the stone excavated to a depth of three feet. His main fear was possibly that others had been there before him, but the problem was not so much grave robbers as the lack of a grave to rob. The site did not appear to have been dug previously, and he concluded that the memorial had been 'brought from some other place, and by vulgar tradition ascribed to Robin Hood'.[17]

Such myths are not easily dispelled however. The stone was regularly attacked by souvenir hunters and by others who believed that pieces of it could cure toothache, and the Armitages subsequently enclosed the site within a low brick wall topped by iron railings and added an inscription. This, couched in pseudo-medieval English and referring to Robin as Earl of Huntingdon, was derived from a poem found among the papers of Thomas Gale, Dean of York from 1697 to 1702:

Hear underneed this laitl stean [Here underneath this little stone]
Lais Robert earl of Huntington [Lies Robert earl of Huntington]
Nea arcir ver as hei sae geud [No archer was as he so good]
An pipl kauld im robin heud [And people called him Robin Hood]
Sick utlaws as hi an is men [Such outlaws as he and his men]
Vil England nivr si agen [Will England never see again]

Gale's verse may itself have been borrowed from a slightly longer and less complimentary version that appeared in Martin Parker's *True Tale of Robin Hood*, published in 1632. Parker claimed, implausibly, that this had been placed on Robin's grave by the Prioress of Kirklees and 'was to bee reade within these hundreth yeares', but he could just as easily have written it himself:

Robert Earle of Huntington
Lies underneath this little stone.
No archer was like him so good:
His wildnesse named him Robbin Hood.
Full thirteene yeares, and something more
These northerne parts he vexed full sore.
Such outlawes as he and his men
May England never know agen.[18]

Parker said that Robin died on 'Decembris quarto die 1198, anno Richardii primi 9', whereas the document found among Gale's papers claimed that he had expired on the 24 kalends of December 1247. The latter date does not exist in the Roman calendar,[19] and it seems unlikely that either man had any real information to impart.

These epitaphs were probably part of a cult of Robin that developed in the seventeenth and eighteenth centuries, and which came to be particularly associated with a well situated at the foot of a hill two miles north-east of the centre of Nottingham. A Robynhode Well near the town is mentioned as early as 1500, and may be identified with a St Anne's Well recorded in 1551, and with the 'Robyn Hood Well alias Saynt Anne Well' noticed forty-six years later.[20] James Brome, whose *Travels over England, Scotland and Wales* was published in 1694, told how he was shown Robin Hood's chair and:

being placed in that chair, we had a cap, which, they say, was his, very formally put upon our heads, and having performed the usual ceremonies befitting so great a solemnity, we receiv'd the Freedom of the Chair, and were incorporated into the Society of that renowned Brotherhood.[21]

A rather fuller description was provided by John Throsby, who visited Nottingham in 1797:

The Well is under an arched stone roof, of rude workmanship, the water is very old, it will kill a toad... It is used by those who are afflicted with rheumatic pains; and indeed, like many other... popular springs, for a variety of disorders. At the house [near the well] were formerly shewn several things said to have belonged to Robin Hood; but they are frittered down to what are now called his cap or helmet and a part of his chair. As these have passed current for many years, and perhaps ages, as things once belonging to that renowned robber, I sketched them.[22]

Throsby drew the two items he mentioned together with the arch and, most remarkably of all, a stone coffin identical to the one Johnston had sketched at Kirklees in 1665. Robin's 'grave' must have been disturbed when Sir Samuel Armitage excavated the site in the early eighteenth century, and the enterprising owners of the well could have acquired it after the dig proved abortive. Brome would surely have mentioned it if it had been displayed when he visited Nottingham in 1694, so it was almost certainly bought or borrowed at some time between then and when Throsby saw it in 1797. There is nothing to indicate what happened to it after the well with its attendant house, pleasure-ground and bowling green, closed as a tourist attraction in the mid-nineteenth century, but adjacent to the north wall of the village church at Loxley in Warwickshire is what may be the same coffin or another exactly like it. Its appearance there may be no more than coincidence, or perhaps someone who had visited the well or seen Johnston's drawing and knew of Robin's connection with the Yorkshire Loxley decided to carve a replica for their own churchyard. But there is a distinct possibility that this is indeed the original graveslab in what must be its third location, and that those who chipped pieces from what they thought was Robin's monument were desecrating an earlier replacement. A drawing made by the Reverend Joseph Ismay, vicar of Mirfield, near Kirklees, in the early 1750s shows a similar, but distinctly different, stone.

The Nottingham well and the arch that protected it should not be confused with a similar spring and canopy that still exist on the east side of the Great North Road, three miles south of Sayles and Wentbridge and a mile south of Barnsdale Bar. Thomas Gent, in his *History of York* written in 1730, mentions 'a very handsome stone arch, erected by the Earl of Carlisle, where passengers from the coach frequently drink'.[23] It was, he says, attended by two servants who, besides dispensing the water, sold souvenirs and regaled travellers with tales of the outlaws. Not far away, on the west side of the road somewhere between the hamlets of Skelbrooke and Wrangbrook (less than a mile from Barnsdale), stood a 'stone of Robert Hode' first recorded in a deed copied into the cartulary of Monk Bretton priory as long ago as 1422. This was clearly a noted landmark – when Henry VII visited the northern parts of his realm in the early months of 1486 he was met by the Earl of Northumberland and a large company of knights and squires drawn from the region at Barnsdale 'a little beyonde Robyn Hoddez ston'.[24] Northumberland had adopted an equivocal, neutral stance at the recent battle of Bosworth, and Professor Pollard suggests that the writer may have been struck by the similarity between the King's gracious acceptance of the Earl's new-found readiness to support him and Robin's pardon in the *Geste*.[25] The stone, which must have been a boundary marker or guidepost, has long since disappeared, but it was apparently the first of the many places to be associated with the outlaw's name.

Little John is said to have retired to Hathersage in north Derbyshire when his swashbuckling days were over, and is associated with a large grave near the church. The stones and railings are modern, but part of an earlier memorial, bearing the weathered initials 'L' and 'I' ('J') may still be seen in the south porch. James Shuttleworth, who owned the manor, excavated the site in 1784, and found a particularly large femur (thigh-bone), 28½ inches long. According to J.W. Walker, he took this home with him and hung it over his bed; but a series of accidents caused him to return it to the local sexton with instructions to replace it in the grave. The sexton decided to exhibit it himself, however, and made a tidy profit until one of his visitors, Sir William Strickland, seized it and carried it away with him. How long Sir William kept it is unknown, but it apparently 'sustained its reputation of bringing ill-luck to the person of its possessor' until he buried it under a tree in his own grounds.[26]

Little John's cuirass of chain mail,[27] together with his bow, arrows and quiver hung in the chancel of Hathersage Church for many years, but were taken to Cannon Hall, near Barnsley, in 1729. The cuirass apparently disappeared when the Hall was being altered in 1778, but J.W. Walker was able to examine the bow which was kept there until the 1970s. It is, he says:

> made of spliced yew, 6 feet 7 inches long, though the ends where the horn tips were attached were broken off. Its girth at the centre is 5 inches, its weight is 21 pounds 2 ounces, and it requires a power of 160 pounds to draw it to its full extent. Carved on the bow is the date 1715 and the name of Colonel Naylor, who in that year had it strung and shot a buck with it at Cannon Park. At that time the two horns at the ends of the bow were perfect. It has never been strung since.[28]

John is also said to have two other graves, one in Ireland where, according to a tradition mentioned by Maurice Keen, he was executed, and another in Scotland. 'In Murray Land', wrote the sixteenth-century chronicler Hector Boece, 'is the Kirke of Pette, quhare the banis [bones] of Lytill Johne remains in gret admiration of pepill. He has bene fourtene fut of hycht... '.[29] Arthur Mee, who visited Blidworth in Nottinghamshire in the course of compiling his *The King's England* series in the 1930s, noted that 'the old men here will tell you that Robin Hood's Will Scarlet lies in the churchyard, and whether it is true or not we think he would have been glad to have this resting-place so near the scenes of his great adventures'.[30] An unusual stone (illustrated), is said to mark the place where he was buried, but is more probably the apex stone of the former church tower. Two cottages, one in Little Haggas Croft at Loxley and the other in Hathersage, were said to be the houses where Robin was born and where Little John spent his last years; but Robin's was ruinous by 1637, and John's was demolished in what are termed 'recent times'. People have always sought to touch the unknowable – to allay their doubts by handling and looking at something that the person they admire might have used or occupied – and there would always have been a tendency for a grave, or bow or tomb that happened to be in the right place or of an appropriate size to be attributed to one of the outlaws. But whether any of them are genuine will never be known.

5

'BAD' KINGS...

The King personified in the Robin Hood ballads was a fair-minded if somewhat blind individual who presided over injustice but was happy to make amends when problems were brought to his attention. His subjects were his children and he wanted only the best for them – or at least that was what outlaws and ordinary people chose to believe. When things went wrong – and they often did – it was not the king who was to blame but ministers and others who gave him bad advice and prevented him from seeing the situation clearly. In 1381, for example, Wat Tyler's rebels murdered the Treasurer and the Archbishop of Canterbury when they occupied London, but never doubted Richard II's word when he offered them pardon and the redress of their grievances. It was precisely this naivety that led the storytellers and their audience to suppose that the king would always forgive Robin, no matter what he had done.

But kings were not like this, of course. Some were 'good' (i.e. able), and others 'bad' (or incompetent), but all were conscious of their authority and directly responsible for what did, or did not, happen. Robin's ruler, whoever he was, would not have taken a personal interest in the activities of a gang of local brigands (unless the threat they posed became disproportionate), and would never have brought himself down to their level. We are dealing with an upside-down world in which criminals stood for justice, kings were kindly and understanding, abusers of authority were punished, and everything (usually) turned out well in the end.

There were five kings who reigned in England in what may be loosely termed the Robin Hood era, Richard I (1189–1199), John (1199–1216), Henry III (1216–1272), Edward I (1272–1307), and Edward II (1307–1327). We will deal with Henry III in chapter seven, but of the others, two, John and Edward II, were, by common consent, among the worst of medieval rulers, while the more capable Richard and Edward I could never have been the 'ideal' king of the ballads. Kings needed to be ruthless and to be feared by their subjects, and there was little peace for those who failed to command respect.

Richard I is unique among English monarchs in that he was a figure of European standing yet played only a small part in the affairs of his own kingdom. His two visits to England after his father, Henry II's, death amounted to only five months in total; and the rest of his 'reign' was spent wandering restlessly about Europe and the Near East fighting battles and conducting negotiations. He saw himself as a ruler of Christendom rather than the monarch of an isolated island kingdom, and it was from this cosmopolitan standpoint that he went on crusade, fought against and forged alliances with Saladin, and settled the affairs of Sicily, Cyprus and Syria along the way. England was little more than a source of finance for his greater enterprises, but he is still remembered as a great soldier and statesman, the archetypal hero king.

Richard, it has been said, combined his father's shrewdness and strength with his mother, Eleanor of Aquitaine's panache and sense of grandeur, and might have been a very able and successful king of England if he had given his mind to it. But he was not prepared to govern personally, and made matters worse by establishing a regency which proved to be unworkable. The two principals, William Longchamp, Bishop of Ely, and Walter of Coutances, Archbishop of Rouen, were both loyal and capable royal servants; but Longchamp, who had risen from humble origins, was widely regarded as a conceited upstart, and his difficulties were compounded by the ambitions of Richard's younger brother Prince John. John, encouraged by the King of France, Philip Augustus, did his best to undermine his brother's position; but the English baronage remained generally loyal to Richard, and the appointment of the more tactful Hubert Walter in place of Longchamp led to greater stability in the latter half of the reign. Walter combined the Justiciership with his role as Archbishop of Canterbury, the first time these two great offices had been brought together in this way.

Richard left England in 1189, and in 1190 arrived in Sicily where he reorganized the government of the island in the aftermath of the death of its ruler, his sister Joanna's husband, William II. This, at first glance, may seem surprising, but Sicily was the 'other' island the Normans had conquered in the 1060s, and both countries had much in common. He also found time to marry his wife Berengaria (a move designed to secure the support of her father, the King of Navarre, against his enemies in France),[1] and did not arrive in Palestine until 1191. Acre was captured, and in September he defeated Saladin at the battle of Arsuf and advanced to within twelve miles of Jerusalem. But the city was well defended, and Richard accepted that to take and hold it was beyond his limited resources. He negotiated a three-year truce (after trying unsuccessfully to marry one of his nieces or a sister into Saladin's family), and then arranged for his nephew, the Count of Champagne, to be elected King of Jerusalem. Guy of Lusignan, the city-state's former ruler, was compensated with Cyprus, which Richard had captured from the Byzantines on his way to the east.

The crusade had failed in its essential purpose – Jerusalem remained in Muslim hands – but Richard was regarded as a hero in many parts of Europe by the time he left Palestine in October 1192. He was aware that John and Philip Augustus were conspiring against him, and so decided to travel home via the Adriatic keeping well to the east of the French king's borders. But it was too late in the year to cross the Alps in comfort, and turning aside to Vienna he was imprisoned by the Duke of Austria, an old enemy of his family. The Duke handed him over to the Emperor, Henry VI, who was only too ready to use him as a bargaining chip in his dealings with his own enemies in Germany,[2] and as a much needed source of funds. Richard was obliged to raise a large ransom (the money being used to finance Henry's conquest of Sicily from his own protégé), and to surrender England which the Emperor then restored to him as an imperial fief.

Richard secured his release early in 1194 and returned to London; but he stayed for only two months before returning to France to pursue his feud with Philip Augustus and remained there for the rest of his life. King Philip had made significant inroads into English-held territory while Richard had been a prisoner, and Richard spent his last years seeking to repair the damage done to his French empire. He reconquered lost lands, built up alliances, constructed castles (most notably the famous Chateau Gaillard which guarded the Seine as it twisted into Normandy), and, as always, planned grandiosely and spent considerably beyond his means. A report that treasure had been found in Limousin persuaded him to attack the town in the hope of solving his financial problems; but during the assault he was wounded in the shoulder by an arrow and died a few days later at the age of forty-one. He left his body to Fontevrault Abbey, his heart to Rouen Cathedral, and his entrails to Charroux in Poitou, but his English kingdom got nothing at all.

So why should a man who was almost wholly a foreigner and who paid such scant attention to England still be regarded as an English, as well as an international, hero? The answer is probably he was always a larger than life character. In his chivalric virtues – and equally in his vices and cruelties – there was nothing average or half-hearted, and the restless, ambitious spirit that had won him fame culminated in his untimely death. He was an absentee ruler whose kingdom had to get along largely without him and who contributed little or nothing to it; but this would have not have mattered to people lower down the social scale who would probably never have seen, or met, him anyway. He was, perhaps, a non-king rather than a bad king, the embodiment of a dream to be admired from afar without probing too deeply beneath the surface. His subjects would have stood in awe of him, even if he seldom concerned himself with them.

King John was one of life's losers. He lost the majority of the lands his immediate predecessors had held in France; he lost his dispute with the Pope over the appointment of Stephen Langton as Archbishop of Canterbury; he lost the argument with his barons and was obliged to grant them a charter of liberties; and he was close to losing his kingdom to a foreign invader when he died in 1216. To most medieval chroniclers and to many nineteenth-century historians he was evil incarnate: but we cannot assume (as they did), that immorality lay at the heart of his troubles or that his failures were entirely his fault.

John was born at Oxford on Christmas Eve 1167, the last of Henry II and Eleanor of Aquitaine's eight children. He was nine years younger than his next brother Geoffrey, ten years younger than the future Richard the Lionheart, and twelve years younger than his eldest surviving brother, the 'Young King Henry'. His prospects seemed decidedly limited (a factor that may have contributed to his apparently negative assessment of his own worth), and his parents may originally have intended him for the priesthood; but any such plan had been abandoned by 1174 when he joined his brother, Henry's household. Here, he would have learned to fight, acquired his later taste for hunting, studied Latin and developed an interest in books. In 1169 Henry II had given his elder sons honorific titles and effectively settled the future partition of his empire among them. But little John 'Lackland' had no place in this scheme of things, and it was not until 1174 that he received the castle and county of Nottingham, the castle and lordship of Marlborough, two castles in Normandy and one each in Anjou, Touraine and Maine. He was given more lands when the Earl of Cornwall died in 1175 (the Earl's daughters had to be content with small grants), and next year was betrothed to Isabella, daughter of the Earl of Gloucester, whose married sisters were effectively disinherited to enrich him.[3]

John was named Lord of Ireland by his father in 1177, but it was not until 1185 when, aged eighteen and newly knighted, he sailed for the territory at the head of a large scale expedition. The campaign was not a success – Gerald of Wales blamed the failure to impose order partly on the immaturity and irresponsibility of John and his young companions – but the death of his brother

Geoffrey in August 1186 increased both his political prominence and the likelihood that he would feature in the succession. Richard demanded, and was refused, recognition as heir-apparent (the 'Young King Henry' had died three years earlier), but his fears that John, who was now closer to their father, might partly or wholly supplant him proved groundless. John was named Count of Mortain in Normandy, confirmed as Earl of Gloucester (he married Isabella in August 1189), and given virtual control over six English counties on Richard's accession: but he appears to have remained uncertain about his future, particularly when Richard named Geoffrey's three year old son Arthur his heir before joining the Third Crusade. He has incurred much criticism for plotting with King Philip during his brother's absence and seeking to prolong his imprisonment; but it must be remembered that Richard had similarly conspired against their father, and had a poor opinion of John's abilities. 'My brother John is not the man to capture a country if there is a single person able to make the slightest resistance to him'[4] he remarked when he heard of his scheming, and accepted John's tearful submission when he returned home. Richard described him as 'childlike', the victim of bad advice and misguided companions, but his contempt, however good-humoured, must have been deeply humiliating to a now twenty-seven year old man.

John was soon restored to his forfeited properties – Richard had no intention of driving him back into the arms of King Philip – and remained loyal to his brother for the rest of his reign. The energy he displayed in helping Richard reconquer lost territory in France, coupled with the fact that Arthur, his rival for the succession, was close to King Philip, considerably enhanced his prospects, and both Hubert Walter and William Marshal (the most powerful lay baron), declared for him in England when Richard died. He was able to reach an agreement with King Philip which gave him nearly all of his father's and brother's French lands subject to certain restrictions, but his position was by no means easy. The debts he had inherited from Richard, and his own military ambitions, caused him to levy unpopular taxes, and Philip was not slow to emphasize his role as feudal overlord and use Arthur's claims to cause him embarrassment. Philip's chance came when the two claimants to the county of La March, Hugh of Lusignan and Isabel of Angouleme, decided to settle their differences by getting married, but were frustrated when the now divorced John seized Isabel and married her himself.[5] The dispossessed Hugh appealed to King Philip who summoned John, also technically his subject, to appear before him; and when John, predictably, refused, Philip announced that he had deprived him of his French fiefs. This would have been an empty threat in Henry II's – and even in Richard the Lionheart's – days, but Philip had gauged John's limitations and was prepared to back his words with force. Normandy was lost to the English crown in 1204, the last castles in Anjou fell in 1205, and in 1206 Philip recovered Brittany aided by the belief that John had murdered Arthur (who was Duke of Brittany in right of his mother), three years earlier. John had captured his nephew in 1202 and imprisoned him first in Falaise and then in Rouen, but there is no real evidence that he was responsible for his death. The Annalist of Margam's story that John killed him in a fit of ungovernable temper and threw his body into the Seine probably tells us more about the rumours that were then circulating than about what actually happened, and a more likely scenario is that Arthur died while attempting to escape.[6] He may have tried to climb from his prison in the castle and fell into the river from a great height.

John tried hard to raise an army in England, but found that his barons were reluctant to become involved in a new war to recover Normandy while his other great problem, his dispute with the papacy, remained unresolved. When Hubert Walter died in 1206 the King was determined to ensure that a reliable royal officer succeeded him as archbishop, and compelled the monks of Canterbury (the 'electors'), to choose his nominee, John de Gray, Bishop of Norwich, although they had already asked the Pope to confirm their own sub-prior in the post. The Pope, Innocent III, confronted by two canonically elected archbishops, declared both their elections invalid, and encouraged the monks to appoint his own candidate, his close friend Stephen Langton. John was furious that his wishes had been disregarded, and when he refused to accept Langton the Pope excommunicated him and placed England under the interdict. Churches were closed for seven years until John finally recognized that he had no alternative but to reach an accommodation with Rome if he was ever to be in a position to deal with his greatest enemy, King Philip. He allowed Langton to take up his see in 1213, and consented to rule England as a papal fief.

As soon as his hands were free, John formed an alliance with his nephew, the German Emperor Otto IV, and planned a joint attack on France. He intended to advance eastwards from Poitou while Otto invaded from Germany, but found that his former Poitivin vassals would no longer support him. King Philip had won their loyalty in the years he had exercised direct authority over the territory, and Otto was decisively defeated at Bouvines on 27 July 1214. A year earlier, some of John's barons had discussed forcing him to govern more moderately and predictably, and his failure in France gave them their opportunity. At first, they had only vague notions of what they wanted; but they remembered Henry I's coronation charter (which listed the abuses Henry had promised to abrogate), and it was this, glossed and amended, which became the basis of the document John was obliged to sign at Runnymede in 1215. The Great Charter, 'Magna Carta', was drawn up in the royal chancery after elaborate consultations between the King and the rebel lords, and under the 'neutral' guidance of Stephen Langton and William Marshal. Its basic premise was that there should be a recognizable body of law governing the relationship between the king and his subjects, and that both were equally bound by it. Initially, it was seen as a plan to deal with an exceptional crisis rather than as a permanent reform of government, but it became a benchmark in the development of both parliament and the constitution itself.

John's view of the Charter was that it was an unwarranted attempt to curb his authority, and he sought to overturn it by any means he could. He persuaded the Pope (now his ally) to condemn it and gathered forces to crush his enemies, but the situation was complicated when King Philip, in an elaborate and somewhat absurd manifesto, announced that he had deposed him and was sending the Dauphin to occupy the English throne. John reacted vigorously, but after a summer and autumn of marching and counter-marching (and after losing his baggage-train in a quicksand at the head of the Wash), he succumbed to illness and died at Newark in October 1216. The barons rallied behind his nine-year-old son Henry, the French challenge was defeated, and the Charter was accepted by all parties by 1225.

John was an arbitrary ruler who lost the support of many of his greatest subjects because he failed to govern in their interests. He might have got away with it if his schemes and wars had been successful, but his failures meant that few had much confidence in him by the time his reign ended. In reality, he was no more ruthless, despotic and immoral than his father and brother; but whereas they were natural leaders of men, John's vassals sometimes refused to fight in his company. The chronicler Roger of Wendover's portrait of a cruel monster who alternated between fits of lethargy and bursts of wild activity is hardly tenable; but John clearly suffered from a defect, or defects, of character, a reputation for inconstancy, that was keenly felt by contemporaries, and which must have some foundation in fact.

Edward I need not long detain us because he was in many ways an able ruler. The wars he waged in Wales, Scotland, and France coupled with his diplomacy, his legislation, his castle-building, and the fact that he was only the second (and the last) English king to actually go on crusade have earned him a high reputation, but even here there was a downside. He may have been 'great' but he was not always 'good', and some aspects of his talents would not be universally admired today.

When Edward succeeded in 1272 the south and east of Wales was divided into several great Marcher lordships, but most of the western half of the principality – Caernarvon, Merioneth, Flint, and much of Denbigh, Montgomery and Radnor – was ruled by Prince Llywelyn ap Gruffydd. The ambitious Llywelyn sought to assert his independence by refusing to perform homage to Edward for his territories, but his defeat in the ensuing war forced him to agree to the Treaty of Conway (1277) which restricted his authority to a much smaller area. One of the subsidiary clauses of the treaty was that property disputes between the Principality and the Marches should be decided by English judges, and the ill-feeling caused by some of their decisions led to renewed conflict and to Llywelyn's death in 1282. The northern and western counties, surrounded by Edward's magnificent ring of fortresses, were henceforth ruled directly by royal administrators, and the 'settlement' endured until Henry VIII's Act of Union in 1536. There is, incidentally, no truth in the story that Edward presented his baby son to the Welsh people as a new 'prince' – the future Edward II was created Prince of Wales when he was seventeen in 1301.

Edward was also successful in Scotland, but here his conquests proved far less enduring. The Scottish kings tacitly acknowledged English overlordship, and when Alexander III died in 1286 Edward arbitrated in the succession in favour of John Balliol. But Balliol was no more willing to be an under-king than Prince Llywelyn, and when he allied with France against England he was deposed and Scotland conquered in 1296. This was the first time that one man had been ruler of all Britain; but the Scots found a popular leader in William Wallace who troubled Edward, as we have seen, until 1305. Edward again briefly governed the whole country, but within months Robert Bruce appeared at the head of a powerful movement of independence and was crowned King of Scotland in March the next year. Edward reacted vigorously, and was about to cross the border in yet another attempt to restore his authority when he died in July 1307. Scotland was his greatest blunder. Its vast areas of wild country made it impossible to quell all the centres of resistance, and the enterprise prevented him from concentrating his energies on richer opportunities for glory in France. Here, the King of England was still Duke of Aquitaine, but the French king, Philip the Fair was determined to exercise effective lordship over the territory much as Edward meant to dominate Scotland and Wales. Philip tried to seize the duchy after Edward refused to appear before him in Paris in 1294, and four years of conflict followed by long negotiations culminated in the marriage of Edward's son, Prince Edward, to Philip's daughter, Isabella, in 1303.

The earlier part of Edward's reign was successful because his resources matched his ambitions, but the higher taxes needed to fight wars in both France and Scotland were resented by those who had to foot the bill. In 1297 the earls forbad the collection of yet another levy because it had been imposed without the consent of a full assembly of knights and burgesses, and two leading magnates, Roger Bigod, Earl of Norfolk, and Humphrey de Bohun, Earl of Hereford, refused to honour their feudal obligation to fight with the King because he proposed sending them to another part of France. 'By God, O Earl, either you go or hang' said Edward, to which the Earl replied – quite correctly as events turned out – 'By the same oath O King, I shall neither go nor hang'. Edward was obliged to confirm Magna Carta and to accept that the 'community of the realm' must assent to all taxation, but the political atmosphere remained one of suspicion even after a truce with France had been concluded. Edward manoeuvred for position, even persuading the Pope to absolve him from his oath confirming the Charter, and his reign closed on this disappointing note.

Edward was respected by his barons, but he was a man of violent temper far removed from the jovial and understanding 'King Edward' of the ballads. On one occasion he paid for the repair of his daughter's coronet after he had damaged it in a fit of anger, and on another gave a page twenty marks after he had assaulted and wounded him at a wedding. It could be argued that Edward blotted his copy-book simply because he lived long enough to do so, and that had he died young – like Henry V for example – our view of him would be quite different. Only a vigorous ruler could bear the burden of kingship – old men could be as much a problem as children – but no medieval monarch retired willingly or allowed his successor to rule in his lifetime. Edward was a ruthless man in a brutal era, an able king but still far from ideal.

Edward II can also be regarded as a 'bad' ruler, but for very different reasons. He resembled his father inasmuch as he was tall, strong, and a good horseman, but he was idle and frivolous, had rather 'unkingly' interests (ditching and acting, for example), and was susceptible to the influence of ingratiating and unscrupulous young men. The barons, who were only too well aware of this, caused him to swear at his coronation that he would govern with the approval of the political community; but his decision to recall the Gascon knight Piers Gaveston (his close friend who his father had expelled from England), confirmed their worst fears. The continuing war with Scotland made Edward dependant on the magnates and Parliament for money, and in March 1310 he was forced to agree to the appointment of a committee of bishops, earls and barons charged with drawing up 'ordinances' regulating the future government of the kingdom. These proposed that Parliament be able to reject a declaration of war, to approve appointments to offices of state and the royal household, and that monies which had previously gone directly to the Wardrobe (i.e. to the King) should henceforward be paid to the Exchequer; but no arrangement that sought to introduce a form of constitutional monarchy could succeed unless the King was prepared to cooperate with it. Edward's view was that the plan placed unwarranted restraints on his personal authority, and differences between the magnates themselves allowed him to avoid submitting to it for the time being.

The progressive decline of English fortunes in Scotland meant that England was not long saddled with the burden of a partial

Previous page: 1. Robin Hood's statue, Castle Green, Nottingham, by James Woodford. Ironically, the robber is sometimes robbed of his arrow and even the lower half of his bow.

Opposite: 2. 'Robyn hod in scherewod stod'. Statue of the outlaw at the Sherwood Forest Visitor Centre.

Above: 3. The Major Oak, Sherwood Forest, named after a Major Rooke who lived locally in the eighteenth century. Robin and his 'merry men' are said to have met beneath its branches.

Right: 4. Robin Hood's Well beside the old Great North Road south of Barnsdale. The arched shelter was erected by the Earl of Carlisle before 1730.

Opposite: 5. St Mary's Church Edwinstowe (Nottinghamshire), where tradition says that Robin and Maid Marian were married.

Above left and right: 6. & 7. Little John's Grave at St Michael's church, Hathersage (Derbyshire), is nearly 14 foot long and is maintained by the Ancient Order of Foresters. The older stone, with its distinctive 'L I' (Little Ihon) is in the church porch.

Below: 8. 'Little John's Well', on the Longshaw Estate (National Trust), near Sheffield. One of several local features associated with the outlaws.

9. Some stones in the churchyard of St Mary of the Purfication, Blidworth (Nottinghamshire), said to mark the place where Will Scarlett was buried. They probably formed part of the tower of the old (now demolished) church.

Below and opposite above: 10. & 11. The apse and south doorway of the Norman chapel at Steetley (Nottinghamshire), where tradition says that Alan a Dale was married and Friar Tuck brought Robin and his men to prayers.

Below: 12. St Mary's Church, Gisburn (Gisborne), Lancashire, presumed home of Sir Guy. The building has changed little since the thirteenth century.

Left: 13. 'Ye Olde Trip to Jerusalem' inn, Nottingham, dating from *c.* 1189. The name recalls the era of the Crusades.

Opposite: 15. Peveril Castle (Derbyshire), built by Henry II, was the administrative centre of the 'Forest of the Peak'.

Below: 14. The remains of 'King John's Palace' at Clipstone (Nottinghamshire), a twelfth-century hunting lodge in the forest.

Above: 17. Granite cross memorial to de Montfort, erected at the expense of Canon Walker, the then vicar, and unveiled by Lord Swinfen, Master of the Rolls, in 1919. The twelfth-century churches of St Lawrence and All Saints are in the background.

Opposite: 16. Simon de Montfort, a portrait in the west window of the Lichfield chapel in All Saints Church, Evesham (Worcestershire), installed in 1883.

Below: 18. Table tomb memorial to Earl Simon on the site of the high altar of Evesham abbey, unveiled by Sir Harry Hylton Foster, Speaker of the House of Commons, in 1965.

Above: 19. 'Battlewell', Green Hill, Evesham, which became a place of pilgrimage in the years after the Earl's death. The algae covered water is barely distinguishable from the surrounding grass.

Opposite: 21. King Richard the Lionheart joins the hands of Robin and Maid Marian. A modern representation of a popular, if unhistorical, legend.

Below: 20. A stone coffin in St Nicholas's churchyard, Loxley, Warwickshire, which may be Robin's. Compare with the drawings made by Nathaniel Johnston at Kirklees in 1665 (see picture 53) and by John Throsby at St Anne's Well in Nottingham before 1797 (see picture 55).

KING RICHARD THE LIONHEART
JOINS THE HANDS OF MAID

ROBIN HOOD AND LITTLE JOHN
FIGHTING ON A BRIDGE

Opposite: 22. Robin and Little John fighting on a bridge.

23. Robin, Marian and Friar Tuck with hounds fighting Guy of Gisborne's men.

24. Edward II. Detail from his tomb effigy in Gloucester Cathedral.

O scicia oscula Lactenus labus uupssa. ñ
inter crebra indicia reprimus inf: q̃ neue
ut pre uer' gr te fili' ñvi albidret cũ
neruf gr patre br di genus imparet.

FR͞ R MATH I͞A S PARISIS͞NS

Matthew Paris, pictured kneeling before the enthroned Virgin and Child (25, *opposite*), described and portrayed many of the events of Henry III's life in his *Chronica Majora* (*this page*, 26, 27, 28, 29).

Right: 30. Henry III, the King opposed by Simon de Montfort, whose troubled reign may have given rise to the Robin Hood stories.

Above: 31. A thirteenth-century drawing of London from the margin of a manuscript of Geoffrey of Monmouth's *History of the Kings of Britain*. London dwarfed all other cities in the kingdom, and control of it was critical to any political cause.

Left: 32. A self-portrait of Geoffrey Chaucer. Chaucer was one of the first to allude to Robin Hood, without specifically naming him, in his *Troilus and Criseyde* (1380).

Below: 33. Magna Carta, the great charter of liberties that King John granted his subjects at Runnymede in June 1215. Autocratic kings like Henry III could not ignore it, and it became the foundation stone of all later attempts at reform.

Opposite: 34. Robin competing in an archery contest, a theme included in three of the four earliest surviving ballads, *Robin Hood and the Potter*, *Robin Hood and Guy of Gisborne*, and a *Little Geste of Robyn Hode and his Meiny* (followers).

Above: 35. Robin and his men move cautiously through the forest. These Victorian prints are inevitably stereotyped, but this one captures the danger of the outlaw life and the ever-present fear of discovery and arrest.

Opposite: 36. Robin and his 'Merry Men' as they are usually portrayed in films and popular literature – relaxed, carefree, and with plenty of time to discover which of them is the best shot!

37. A lady, her son, and an abbot ride through the forest. They were aware of the danger of ambush – hence the guards – but had little choice but to pass through high-risk areas when the path took them that way.

38. Robin, disguised as a potter, gives the last of his borrowed pots to the sheriff's wife. It was a popular story-line found in tales told of other outlaws, notably Hereward the Wake and Eustace the Monk.

39. Friar Tuck was a real person, at least in the sense that Robert Stafford, a chaplain of Linfield, in Sussex, borrowed or coined the name when he led an outlaw band in the early fifteenth century. In *Robin Hood and the Curtal Friar,* he is obliged to carry Robin across a river.

40. Robin agrees to help a poor knight who is journeying to York to plead with the abbot of St Mary's for more time to repay his debt, and allows Little John to act as his squire. A story from the *Geste*.

41. A monk of St Mary's abbey is captured by the outlaws and is found to have exactly double the amount owed by the knight in his possession. He is relieved of his money and the story ends happily – for Robin and the knight!

42. The king of the ballads is always chivalrous and ready to forgive when the situation is explained to him, but most rulers would have been more inclined to hang Robin and his men than pardon them. Here, he reveals himself to the outlaws in a scene from the *Geste*.

43. The abbess of Kirklees deceitfully lures an apprehensive Robin to his death. Robin had asked her to bleed him to cure his sickness, and had dismissed warnings that she was up to no good.

44. Robin Hood as he is often seen in childrens' books, wearing clothes that are two or three centuries too late for the real Robin.

45. An old story-teller and a young listener, an engraving by Thomas Berwick, c. 1795, from J. Ritson, *Robin Hood: A Collection of all the Ancient Poems, Songs and Ballads, now extant, Relative to the Celebrated English Outlaw*, 2 vols. (1887). The stories may have been retold and revised on many occasions before the final (printed) versions emerged.

46. Robin Hood fighting Guy of Gisborne (Berwick in Ritson). Guy is Robin's bitterest enemy after the Sheriff of Nottingham, although we are never told why.

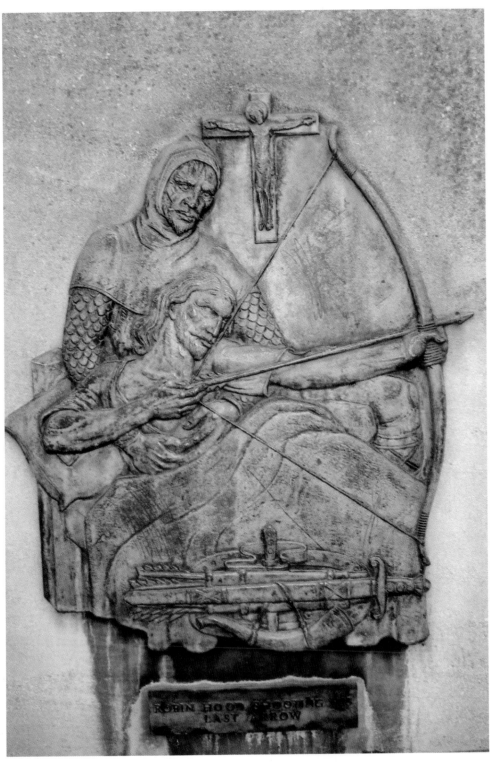

Above and next page: 47 & 48. The dying Robin, supported by Little John, prepares to shoot an arrow indicating where he wants to be buried after his betrayal by the prioress and his battle with Sir Roger of Doncaster at Kirklees priory.

conquest, but the defeat of Bannockburn in the summer of 1314 brought a renewed sense of crisis to the reign. The most powerful magnate, Earl Thomas of Lancaster (who had not been present at Bannockburn and who had not, therefore, been tainted by the debacle), used the parliaments of September 1314 and January 1315 to insist on the enforcement of the Ordinances, and at the Lincoln parliament of 1316 gained the formal position of chief councillor with the right to act jointly with the King. Unfortunately, he lacked Edward's friendship, the one asset that might have made cooperation in government possible, and after two years was supplanted by a new group of counsellors – most notably the Earls of Pembroke and Hereford and Hugh Despenser the Younger – who had gained the King's confidence since 1314. These formed a 'middle' party in the sense that they aimed neither at the rule of a single, all-powerful courtier, like the now deceased Gaveston, nor at destroying the Edward's independence from outside, like Lancaster; and they came to an agreement with Earl Thomas (the Treaty of Leek, August 1318), by which he surrendered his former right of veto in return for the enforcement of the Ordinances and the establishment of a council to 'manage' the King.

This arrangement might well have enabled Edward to proceed to the end of his reign without further mishap had it not been for the ambitions of Hugh Despenser the Younger. Between 1318 and 1321 Despenser used his position as royal chamberlain to enlarge his personal authority, ordered judges to rule in his favour in legal disputes, and ultimately refused to allow the King to see anyone unless he was present. His influence over Edward roused Thomas of Lancaster and some lords of the Welsh Marches (whose lands Despenser coveted) to insist on his removal; but the King was still able to command considerable support among the magnates and their campaign ended with Earl Thomas's execution after Boroughbridge in 1322. A parliament summoned to York revoked the Ordinances, and Edward was vindicated as never before.

A wiser king might have behaved magnanimously in the aftermath of victory, but Edward's executions, imprisonments and forfeitures engendered a legacy of bitterness that would ultimately destroy him. Hugh Despenser was granted estates which could have been used to create a new, loyal following, and his power and arrogance won him enemies on all sides. In fairness to him it must be said that he made peace with Scotland and carefully reorganized the Crown's finances; but none of this endeared him to the barons or to Isabella, Edward's queen. Isabella bitterly resented the homosexual nature of Despenser's relationship with her husband, and she and their twelve-year-old son Edward signally failed to return to England after performing homage for Aquitaine in 1325. She began a liaison with Roger Mortimer, a disaffected baron who had escaped to the Continent, and when they landed in Suffolk in September 1326 with a force of Flemish mercenaries they were joined by sympathizers who included the King's half-brothers, the Earls of Kent and Norfolk, and Henry, Thomas of Lancaster's brother and heir. Resistance collapsed, Edward was captured, and Despenser was executed in a particularly brutal way.

The Parliament that met in January 1327 carried through the first deposition of a reigning king since the Conquest. Edward was obliged to abdicate in his son's favour at Kenilworth, and was murdered at Berkeley Castle in September. Roger Mortimer, created Earl of March, was now effectively in charge of the young King's government, but he proved to be as acquisitive and unpopular as Hugh Despenser. Several conspiracies against him were thwarted (the Earl of Kent was executed and Earl Henry forced into submission), but Edward III himself resolved the situation when he seized Roger in Nottingham Castle on the night of 19 October, 1330. The Earl was executed and Edward began his personal reign.

Edward II's great fault was his weakness of character, evident both in his dependence on favourites (fatal in terms of his inability to manage the system of royal patronage), and in his over-reaction in the aftermath of Boroughbridge. Some indication of the numbers executed or imprisoned was given in chapter three; and unlike the period after Evesham (see chapter 9), the fines for restitution were large and arbitrary, not set at pre-determined rates. The Crown's new-found wealth, and the conclusion of the costly war with Scotland, meant that the barons could no longer restrain or influence the King by withholding taxes, and resulted in their almost total exasperation with his mismanagement. The system did not allow incompetent rulers to be dismissed from office, and such men had either to be tolerated or deposed when they became insufferable. There may have been no 'ideal' kings (ideal, that is, from everyone's perspective), but some of these were clearly worse than most.

6

... & 'GOOD' OUTLAWS

Kings were, after all, only men, and no one should be surprised if some of them abused their power and privileges or were otherwise found wanting. What is more unusual is that outlaws who readily murdered people to obtain money that did not belong to them were regarded not as the criminals they undoubtedly were but as popular heroes. Professor Stones notes how many contemporary documents bear witness that:

> all over England, disturbers of the peace are said to gather together daily to do evil; they ride in force by day and night taking and robbing people at their will, imprisoning some of them until they have made grievous (or sometimes 'intolerable') ransoms. They form congregations and illicit conventicles [unlawful assemblies], and wander in woods and other public and private places, ambushing wayfarers whom they rob and sometimes slay. In all these things they are aided and abetted by local people, who incite them to their evil deeds and shield them after they are done.[1]

The careers of two gangs who operated in the first half of the fourteenth century – the Folvilles and the Coterels – have been well documented,[2] and help to explain why such evidently unsavoury characters could be seen in a surprisingly favourable light.

The Folvilles were the sons of John de Folville, lord of Ashby Folville in Leicestershire and Teigh in Rutland, who died in 1310. John, the eldest, inherited Ashby Folville manor and lived the conventional life of a country squire; but his six brothers (Eustace, Laurence, Richard, Robert, Thomas and Walter), were habitual criminals. Among their more notorious offences was the murder of Roger Bellars, baron of the Exchequer, in January 1326, and the kidnapping and ransoming of Sir Richard Willoughby, justice of the King's Bench, in 1332. One, at least, came to a sticky end. The Reverend Richard de Folville was cornered in his church at Teigh by Sir Robert Colville, and shot one of his pursuers dead and wounded several others before he was dragged out and beheaded.[3] But Eustace, the leader of the gang, against whom there were five outstanding charges of murder besides a score of other felonies, was pardoned in 1333 in recognition of the good service he had rendered in the Scottish war and on condition that he would make himself available if summoned again.

One reason the brothers were never convicted, still less punished, for their misdemeanours was that, for a time at least, they were on the winning side of the argument. The Despenser-dominated government threatened them with arrest for the murder of Bellars in 1326 – they were even excluded from the reconciliation offered to those who would join the fight against Roger Mortimer and Queen Isabella – and unsurprisingly, they were pardoned soon after the Queen and her lover seized power. Edward III's overthrow of Mortimer in 1330 again placed them in jeopardy, but they seem to have had little difficulty avoiding capture while they earned his favour. It is significant that Eustace's 1333 pardon omitted the standard 'saving our suit against those who capture and detain people of our realm until they have paid ransoms at their (i.e. their captors') will',[4] and meant that he could not now be arraigned for his part in the mistreatment of Justice Willoughby. He was a rogue, but a useful man to have on your side.

The indulgence of the central government was advantageous but not essential. Another factor in the Folvilles' success was that in difficult times they were able to hide with powerful like-minded friends like John de Vere, the Constable of Rockingham Castle, who had once faced down a royal justice and ambushed the Abbot of Pipewell. The indictment against him alleges that:

> sometimes twenty armed men, sometimes thirty, come to Vere at the castle, and they leave at dawn, or during the night. He shuts the gates on the side facing the town, and they can leave secretly, by a postern [side gate]. Those bringing victuals to the castle are not allowed to enter, lest they should come to know those armed men.[5]

De Vere and others protected the Folvilles much as Sir Richard at the Lee protected Robin, and they were unlikely to be brought to justice as long as some of those responsible for upholding the law in the localities had a foot in both camps.

The Folvilles were not the sort of men anyone would necessarily wish to encounter, but their activities met with a measure of approval in some unlikely quarters. The chronicler Henry Knighton describes Richard de Folville as a 'fierce, daring and impudent' man, adjectives more applicable to a popular hero than a feared criminal. In Knighton's opinion, Roger Bellars had provoked the Folvilles, and it was hardly coincidence that Justice Willoughby was afterwards fined £1,000 by Edward III on the grounds that he had 'sold the laws of England as though they had been oxen or cattle'.[6] Professor Stones suggests that 'many people took a fairly light-hearted view of the Folvilles' crimes and were far from friendly to the powers who sought to arrest them'.[7] The outlaw appeared to have right on his side.

The Coterel gang – James, John and Nicholas Coterel and their associates – joined the Folvilles in capturing and ransoming Willoughby, although they usually operated separately in Nottinghamshire and Derbyshire. They were already noted for their lawlessness when they murdered Sir William Knyveton and John Maykynson at Bradley (Derbyshire) in June 1330, but again, bringing them to book proved all but impossible. A local rival, Roger de Wennesley, was ordered to arrest them but instead threw in his lot with them,[8] and their influential supporters included the knights William Aune of Gringley (Nottinghamshire), Robert Tuchet of Mackworth (Derbyshire), and, more surprisingly, Robert Ingram, the sheriff and sometime member of Parliament who was mentioned as a possible candidate for Robin Hood's sheriff in chapter four. Again, it seems highly irregular that a man charged with maintaining the law should collude with those who were breaking it, but Ingram was far from being the exception. Outlaws could find a corrupt sheriff or judge a useful ally when there was nowhere to hide.

One reason that these supposed pillars of society were prepared to help bandits like the Folvilles and Coterels was that they found it financially advantageous to do so. When the two gangs combined to seize Justice Willoughby, the Folvilles received only 300 of the 1,300 marks ransom, and the Coterels a mere 40. What happened to the rest is unknown, but it presumably found its way into the pockets of men like de Vere and Tuchet whose connivance allowed both gangs to operate with impunity. William Amyas, a former mayor of Nottingham and the second richest man in the town, was told that his property would be burned in he did not pay £20 'protection money', and double this amount was demanded from the wealthy Sir Geoffrey Lutterell whose son-in-law, Geoffrey le Scrope, Chief Justice of the King's Bench, was one of the outlaws' principal adversaries. The Coterels were able to arrange for food – and even their rents – to be brought to them in the woods on occasion, and, in the words of the Bakewell jurors 'rode armed publicly and secretly in manner of war by day and night'.[9] It was a lucrative business, but toleration came at a price.

In the end the Coterels, like the Folvilles, seem to have made their peace with the authorities, thanks mainly to Edward III's decision to wage war in both Scotland and France. Men who proved themselves willing and able soldiers were unlikely to have their past crimes examined too closely, and it is no coincidence that James Coterel, the leader of the gang, and Sir William Aune, his one-time protector, both received royal appointments later in the decade. James was instructed to pursue and arrest a miscreant Leicestershire parson in November 1336, while Aune was commissioned to survey decaying castles in Wales in 1334 and to requisition ships for a Scottish expedition three years later. Another member of the gang, William de Uston, was sentenced to death in September 1332 (he was one of the few ever to be convicted), but was clearly back in favour when he was appointed to investigate certain murders at Leicester in 1341. No one seems to have thought it incongruous that he had been on the wrong side of the law himself.

The one exception was Nicholas Coterel who became Queen Philippa's bailiff of the High Peak (Derbyshire). He interfered in the collection of a parliamentary subsidy in October 1337, and when he was ordered to lead sixty archers recruited in the bailiwick to Scotland 'stealthily withdrew without licence converting the wages of the men to his own use as well as sums he levied from the queen's tenants for the chattels of fugitives and felons and from the queen's fees'.[10] We do not know if he subsequently chose the path of righteousness, but it would not be surprising if he did so. His fellow poachers turned gamekeepers all found royal service more rewarding than life on the road.

The Folvilles and the Coterels are the two best-documented gangs of the early fourteenth century, but they were far from alone. Outlaws were always obliged to live by their wits, and it is no surprise to find them operating in other places and at other times. The pass at Alton in Hampshire (on the main road between Winchester and London), became notorious as a haunt of robbers in the mid-thirteenth century, so much that in 1269 the Justices in Eyre petitioned the King to clear and widen the road to make ambushes more difficult. We do not know if this was done or if crime in the area subsequently diminished, but the wardens of the annual St Giles fair at Winchester employed five mounted guards in the fourteenth century, and Langland remarked ironically in *Piers Plowman* that only Poverty could go there in safety. It was probably at Alton that a pageant designed to surprise, and amuse, the captive King John of France was staged in 1357. The writer of the *Anomialle Chronicle* tells of how, as the royal party passed 'near a forest', it was intercepted by 500 men dressed in green posing as robbers. The King asked the Black Prince, who was riding with him, to explain their behaviour, and the Prince replied that 'they were English foresters living in the wild and that it was their custom to do this every day'.[11] It was a parody of a scene that must have been acted out many times on a smaller scale over the years.

Later gangs who employed much the same tactics included one led by William Beckwith which operated in Knaresborough forest (Yorkshire), between 1387 and 1392. Beckwith was popularly said to have been betrayed and murdered by one Thomas Blande at Barnard Castle much as Robin Hood was betrayed at Kirklees; but the chronicler was unaware that Blande, a trusted employee of the lord of Barnard, was more likely to have been an enemy of outlaws than a false friend. Robert Stafford ('Friar Tuck') and his band were accused of robberies and murders besides poaching from local warrens on the Sussex-Surrey border in about 1417, and Piers Venables and his men, who operated in the vicinity of Tutbury (Staffordshire) in the late 1430s, were likened to 'Robin Hood and his meynie' in an official complaint. Matters were no better later in the century when an Alan Greneside and two accomplices ambushed a passing jeweller at Wentbridge in September 1466 and relieved him of £80 in money and valuables, or when William Robinson, a labourer, and others held up a canon between Pontefract and Wentbridge and stole a casket containing £400 in May 1472.[12]

These robbers all flouted the law and never gave any of their ill-gotten gains to poorer people, but they were nevertheless admired in many quarters. The Coterels were sustained by those who brought them food as well as by more highly placed supporters, while the Folvilles enjoyed a measure of popular approval they never earned by 'good' deeds. By the time Langland wrote *Piers Plowman* in 1377, 'Folville's laws' had become a byword for the (entirely justifiable) redress of grievances by force:

And some to ryde and to recovere that unrightfully was wonne:

He wissed hem wynne it ayein [back] thorough wightnesse [strength]

of handes,

And fecchen it fro false men with Folvyles lawes.[13]

The implication was clearly that those who could not obtain redress through the laws of England could appeal instead to the law of Folville. Rough justice could, and sometimes did, replace royal justice when corruption in the traditional system was rife.

There has always been a tendency for government officials to line their own pockets at the expense of others, but such abuses may have worsened when the Despensers held sway over Edward II and when Edward III needed money to wage his wars (wars that took him away from the centre of government), in the 1330s. It is probably no coincidence that it was precisely at these times that the Coterel and Folville gangs flourished, but it is still remarkable that those who blatantly flouted the law should become the guardians of a popular alternative to it. Perhaps it was inevitable that when royal officials were obviously dishonest and grasping, those who opposed them – for the best or the worst of reasons – would become heroes to ordinary people. Dr Maddicott has written that 'when taxation was excessive, venality ubiquitous and sheriffs particularly corrupt, the outlaw's resort to self-help is likely to have been viewed with more than usual sympathy'.[14] Members of modern-day parliaments should take note!

It would be easy to romanticize the careers of men like the Folvilles and Coterels, but romance and reality are often quite different. These were ruthless men, men whose commitment to extortion and readiness to kill when it suited them are reflected in the Robin Hood ballads, but who lacked the redeeming features that make the Robin of legend a more appealing figure. They were more concerned to settle scores with old enemies and enrich themselves in the process than to display exaggerated politeness or piety, but they would not have rejected popular approval of their activities and may even have encouraged it. We can never be sure if they were consciously acting as dispensers of 'rough justice' or whether they were merely cocking a snook at authority. But however they saw themselves, it is clear that they won popular support because, like Thomas of Lancaster and others, there was a general perception that they were prepared to right wrongs that could not be righted by any constitutional or legal method. Today, we would criticize them for using violence, but medieval people did not see it in quite this way. The law itself frequently resorted to violent solutions, and if an objective was just, so too were the means of attaining it. In Professor Pollard's words, 'this is exactly what Robin Hood celebrates – righteous violence to maintain true justice precisely when the officers of the law have failed'.[15]

But if the outlaws were actively seeking to combat injustice, they were not seeking to change either the system or society. It is no coincidence that the only really successful rebels were men like the Folvilles and Coterels, who operated locally and whose main purpose was to line their own pockets. 'National' insurgents like Wat Tyler, Jack Cade and Robert Kett enjoyed initial success, but failed because they thought only in terms of kings, aristocrats and judges. They had no concept of an alternative, or 'better', society, and would have been content if the kings, aristocrats and judges had treated them fairly. Maurice Keen has pointed out that the qualities that made Robin and other outlaws heroes of the people would have made them 'just lords' within the existing system. 'The final solution was not a new dispensation but a change of personnel'.[16]

The leaders of the Folvilles, Coterels and other gentry bands also preferred to *use* the existing system rather than think in terms of dismantling it. Sheriffs, juries and witnesses could all be bought or threatened, and the gangs were unlikely to try to change an arrangement that quite literally allowed them to get away with murder. The only justification for their behaviour is that this was a harsh world in which everyone carried weapons and violence was commonplace. Life was cheap and cruelty endemic, although not (usually) mindless or gratuitously sadistic. Roger Bellars was singled out because, according to Knighton, he had threatened and injured the Folvilles, and Little John and Much the Miller's son killed the monk's young page to prevent him from identifying them. Their way of living had made them callous, and it was survival – their own rather than someone else's – that came first.

But why did men like the Folvilles and Coterels resort to a life of crime in the first place? The ballads say nothing of how or why Robin became an outlaw, so can any clues be gleaned from the careers of others? On one level, the bandits had scores to settle with people who *were* the law and who were effectively immune from prosecution, but there seems little doubt that the main motive was financial. The Folvilles were all younger sons who would inherit nothing unless something happened to their eldest brother (and not even then if he left children), and robbery and extortion provided them with a better income that they could have obtained by other, more legitimate methods. It is almost certainly no coincidence that they abandoned their wayward lives in the later 1330s when the King's wars offered them both regular employment and the prospect of booty and ransoms. It was the offer of a job in the royal household that persuaded Robin to desert the greenwood (at least temporarily), and it is possible that he did not *choose* to lead the life of an outlaw in the first place. An accused who was summoned to appear before a county court and failed to attend because he doubted he would be treated fairly would have been obliged to hide and survive by whatever means were available to him. Robbery – and the violence that accompanied it – would have become a necessity, a way of life.

There are a number of parallels between Robin and the gangs mentioned above. The Coterels, to quote Professor Bellamy:

> poached, ambushed, had a spy in Nottingham, ill-treated clerics, were pursued by bounty hunters and the sheriff, operated in Sherwood, entered royal service, had as an ally a member of the gentry who had lost his inheritance [Sir William Aune], and were pardoned by the king.[17]

It sounds almost as though one could be the other, but there are also a number of subtle differences. Robin did not join forces with other gangs or sell his services to those who wanted to avenge a wrong or threaten a rival (unlike the Folvilles and Coterels who were always 'guns for hire'), nor did he apparently form an alliance with anyone in any kind of authority except for the poor knight. The Folvilles and others were not expert archers (unless the accounts of their deeds wholly omit the fact), and they were certainly not courteous, be it to one another or to those they robbed. The ballads reflect some typical outlaw activity, but they have a dimension that is peculiarly their own.

In sum, it may be fairly said that outlaws were never 'good' in the true sense of the word, nor were the kings who reigned over them wholly 'bad'. The deeds that made the outlaws into popular heroes stemmed from the fact that some of their victims were corrupt and disliked by sections of the populace; but their 'rough justice', however desirable, was always brutal and arbitrary, and the very antithesis of the careful, even-handed judgements of a sound legal system. The Kings were well aware of what was happening, but could do little about it. The practice whereby Justices in Eyre made regular visitations and held dishonest sheriffs and others to account began to collapse after about 1300 (probably because the small number of professional judges could not cope with the workload), and although some of their duties were taken over by commissions of gaol delivery (which tried all the prisoners in a specific gaol), and commissions of oyer and terminer (charged with dealing with a wave of crime in a particular area), they were less successful in limiting the malpractices of royal officials. The problem, of course, was that once justice was seen to be partial, plaintiffs and defendants were obliged to resort to violent or dishonest means to win their cases. Professor Bellamy has pointed out how men might commit offences when an opportunity for profit or revenge presented itself, 'but then revert back to obedience to the law, even to upholding it, for the rest of the year, the decade, or even a lifetime'.[18] When several members of the royal household were executed for helping to rob two merchants at the pass of Alton in 1248, they asked the hangman to tell the King that he was responsible for their deaths because the late payment of their wages had forced them to resort to such measures! Some departures from the straight and narrow were arguably, justified, but we should not romanticize the perpetrators or suppose that they represented anyone's interests but their own.

7

HENRY III & SIMON DE MONTFORT

We omitted Henry III from our discussion of the kings who have been associated with Robin Hood because, as we shall see, the man whose career contributed most to the legend of Robin actually lived in his reign. Henry's youth on his accession in 1216 meant that he could not govern unaided, but it is possible to argue that his relative weakness was also conversely, his greatest strength. Although he was John's son he had no personal enemies, and he could rely on the shrewd guidance of the papal legate, Cardinal Guala, and William Marshal. Within two years they had united the warring factions, compelled the Dauphin to abandon his ambition to rule England, and ended the confusion that had closed John's reign. Guala returned to Rome in 1218 and Marshal died in 1219; but their mantles were taken up by the Justicier, Hubert de Burgh, and by Archbishop Langton. The result was that England was peaceful and prosperous at the beginning of 1227 when Henry began to rule personally at the age of nineteen.

Henry, like his exemplar Edward the Confessor, was artistic and religious, but he lacked the strength and ruthlessness that had characterized his immediate predecessors. Of sturdy, medium build, with a drooping eyelid, he has been described as accessible, affable and courteous; but he was indifferent to hunting and tournaments and preferred a sedentary, comfortable life to the rigours of kingship. He might feed 500 paupers and hear mass four times daily, but these were not substitutes for an ability to command and to earn the respect of his greatest subjects. The chronicler of Osney Abbey described him as 'simplex', but did he mean that he was honest and straightforward (the usual translation of the word), or foolish and easily led?

Henry wanted to be a 'great' ruler like his grandfather, Henry II, and his uncle, Richard the Lionheart, but the loss of Normandy and the restraints imposed by Magna Carta meant that his situation was very different to theirs. He still had considerable freedom in vital areas of policy (in making appointments, for example), but failed to realize that most of his barons had accepted the loss of their French lands when they committed themselves to England in 1204. They were unwilling to wage war against an obviously more powerful enemy, an attitude that did not endear them to Henry who could be obstinate or petulant according to his mood. He came to treat those who should have been his closest advisers with suspicion, and although the quiet simplicity of his nature helped him endure the miseries and failures of his reign without bitterness he was never an ideal king.

Henry's adult reign falls into two parts: the period from 1229 to 1258 when he was effectively in charge of the government, and the period after 1258 when real power was sometimes exercised by committees of barons and ultimately by Edward, his son. The barons tried to influence – and ultimately to control – the King, while Henry tried to maintain the near-absolutism of his predecessors: but they never thought in terms of deposing him – still less of abolishing the monarchy – even when he was a prisoner and some of them ruled in his name. The royal court was the centre of English politics, and everyone thought of government in terms of royal government: but there was a growing debate about how the great power of the Crown should be exercised, and failures in royal policy gave critics both the excuse and the opportunity they needed. The barons had become accustomed to a consultative role in government (they had been regularly consulted during the royal minority), and disliked the way in which Henry regularly sought advice from his personal – usually foreign – favourites rather than from them.[1] It was traditional for the great men of the kingdom, lay and clerical, to meet together in a Great Council to advise the King on important issues: but the composition and frequency of the Council lay entirely within the royal prerogative, and the sovereign was not obliged to confer with his magnates – or take their advice – unless he thought it appropriate. This was perfectly acceptable while the King used his powers judiciously and the barons had confidence in him; but Henry was not judicious, and the barons (who knew that he dreamed of recovering his grandfather and uncle's French empire), feared that he would commit them to foreign adventures with potentially disastrous consequences. He was a man to be watched.

The first foreigners to gain Henry's favour were the Poitevins Peter des Roches, Bishop of Winchester, and his son or nephew, Peter des Rivaux, who were instrumental in forcing Hubert de Burgh from office. Henry married Eleanor of Provence (Louis IX's wife's sister) in 1236, and after des Roches fell from power turned increasingly to her uncles, William, Peter and Boniface of Savoy. Peter was created Earl of Richmond while Boniface became Archbishop of Canterbury, and the situation worsened when Henry invited his half-brothers, Aymer, William, Guy and Geoffrey, his mother's sons by her second marriage to Hugh of Lusignan, to come to England in 1247. More titles followed – William became Earl of Pembroke and Aymer Bishop of Winchester – and the court was divided not only by English distaste for the aliens but by rivalries among the different groupings. The Savoyards gained acceptance over time, but the Lusignans were always a step too far.

Henry's middle years witnessed several disputes that a wiser king would have avoided, not least when he allowed his sister Eleanor to marry the French adventurer, Simon de Montfort (another of his young foreign friends), in 1238. Simon was to become one of the best known figures in English history, but he should not be confused with his equally famous father and namesake who had been killed leading the Albigensian Crusade against the Cathar heretics in 1218. Simon the elder was the son of one of two co-heiresses of the last Beaumont Earl of Leicester and would have become a great lord in England in other circumstances: but his commitment to the French crown had prevented him from claiming his share of the lands and they had been granted to a series of 'keepers' after his uncle died.[2] The younger Simon, born about 1208, was only his father's third son and had few prospects in his native France; but shortly before 1230 he persuaded his eldest brother, Amaury, to allow him to cross to England to seek the family's moiety of the Leicester inheritance. Both Amaury and the keeper of the lands, the elderly Earl of Chester, had to be compensated, of course; but Simon's petition was successful and he became a junior member of Henry III's court.

Henry's generosity in giving Simon estates to which he had some claim does not seem to have upset the English establishment, but allowing him to wed his sister was an entirely different matter.

Eleanor had been a widow since her first husband William Marshal, the great William Marshal's son, had died in 1231, and the barons fully expected that her brother would marry her to someone whose connections would be of real benefit to England.[3] Henry subsequently claimed that de Montfort had seduced Eleanor and that he had agreed to a hurried, almost secret, wedding to avoid a scandal, but his readiness to facilitate the arrangement would not suggest that it had been forced upon him. He wrote to the Pope asking him to look favourably on Simon when he went to Rome to seek confirmation of the union, and faced down Edmund, Boniface of Savoy's predecessor as Archbishop of Canterbury, before whom Eleanor had taken a vow of chastity. It was another case of the King failing to consult when he ought to have consulted, and treating an important state matter like a private family concern.

How did Simon achieve this? Henry was probably influenced by his personal charisma and particularly his 'pleasant and courteous way of speaking'[4], but a more practical consideration was surely that a ruler who dreamed of re-conquering Normandy and Poitou needed capable generals familiar with continental warfare. Simon was perhaps fortunate that he arrived in England at the moment that Henry was about to embark on his first unsuccessful attempt to recapture Normandy, and his marriage to Eleanor may reflect the extent to which the King had come to rely upon him eight years later. It may be an exaggeration to suggest that Simon played Buckingham to Henry's Charles I, but Henry undoubtedly admired his natural ability and authority and may have secretly wished he possessed such qualities himself.

Eleanor's large dower from her first husband secured Simon's financial position when he was created Earl of Leicester in 1239,[5] but by then he was heavily in debt. His Leicester estates were worth around £500 per annum, but this was not enough to meet his obligations – to buy out rival claims to his inheritance while maintaining his status as a great nobleman – and led to his first serious quarrel with the King. He had borrowed significant sums of money to make ends meet, and when one of his creditors, Thomas of Savoy (another of the Queen's uncles), sued him in the papal curia, he told Thomas that Henry would guarantee the debt. Henry had not agreed to this however – Simon had simply assumed that his brother-in-law would help him – and was predictably furious when he found out. Simon only narrowly escaped being committed to the Tower, and sought refuge from the King's anger in France.

Henry was often temperamental but he did not bear grudges. He received Simon affably when the Earl briefly crossed to England in 1240 to raise funds for the crusade he had planned to undertake before their quarrel, and again summoned him to his side when he returned from the Holy Land in 1242. Another attempt to recover Poitou was getting into difficulties, and although Simon lost no time in joining the English army he could do little more than help cover its retreat. Henry was probably astounded when Simon told him that he deserved to be locked up, like Charles the Simple, imprisoned after the battle of Soissons in 923; but he still rewarded him generously when they returned to England. Some £2,000 worth of his debts were cancelled, he was given the great castle of Kenilworth (Warwickshire) which was to become his principal home, and was exempted from the feudal taxation imposed in 1245. Henry disliked, perhaps even feared, his sometimes angry outbursts, but he was both a member of the royal family and too valuable an ally to be dismissed.

The majority of English magnates had been opposed to the campaign in Poitou, and they became still more disgruntled when Henry tried to recoup his financial losses – and pay for his extravagant building works – by a series of harsh measures designed to raise cash. His demands fuelled the debate that it ought to be possible to restrict the royal authority in the interests of good government, and the so-called 'Paper Constitution' preserved by Matthew Paris (sometimes said to date from as early as 1238 but usually assigned to 1244), may not be the only such scheme devised in these years. It proposed that 'four men of rank and power shall be chosen by common consent from the most discreet persons of the whole realm to be of the king's council, to handle the affairs of the king and of the kingdom and do justice to all without respect of persons'. They were to manage 'the lord king's treasure', spending it 'for the benefit of the king and the kingdom as they think best', approve the appointment of officials including the justicier and chancellor, and were to have authority to remove 'those thus far suspect and not needed' from the King's side.[6] We do not know if these ideas were ever put to Henry or, if they were, how he responded to them, but nothing could be done without his approval. The magnates never wanted weak royal government – on the contrary, they wanted an effective government in which affairs were conducted on the basis of a harmonious understanding between the king and his greatest subjects and in a rational and orderly manner. The problem was that kings who were too inept to rule effectively never realized that they needed good advice.

Henry and Simon's relationship was based on their ultimate dependence on one another, but the differences in their personalities meant that a crisis could develop at any moment. In 1248 the King sent his brother-in-law to Gascony in south-western France (where Henry was still nominally duke) with authority to reduce the turbulent territory to order. Simon set about his task with his usual ruthless efficiency, and it was not long before Gascon noblemen were complaining that he was ignoring their traditions and, more worryingly, that he meant to carve out a principality for himself. There was no truth in the stories as Henry should have realized, but he decided to summon all the parties to England and subjected Simon to what amounted to a trial. Simon argued persuasively that his accusers were either wrong or that his severity was entirely justified, and was vindicated when it became clear that a majority of the English barons sympathized with him. In the end, Gascony was tamed and he was again well rewarded for his efforts; but the episode proved to him that he could not trust the King to act with sense and consistency or recognize base slanders against his friends.

Simon and the barons were effectively stuck with Henry, but he might have floundered on to the end of his reign without more than occasionally annoying them if he had not become involved in a scheme to place his younger son, Edmund, on the throne of Sicily in 1254. The Emperor Frederick, whose rule in both Germany and south Italy had threatened the security of the Papal States from two directions, had died in 1250, and the Pope, Innocent IV, resolved to break the German stranglehold by giving the Sicilian crown (which was theoretically within his gift) to another family. He cast about Europe for a suitable candidate – someone close to a throne who could harness his national resources to drive the Germans from south Italy – but his first choices, Richard of Cornwall, King Henry's brother, and Charles of Anjou, Louis IX's brother, both rejected his offer. Richard of Cornwall went so far as to say that the Pope 'might as well have asked him to climb into the skies and capture the moon';[7] but his fears were entirely lost on King Henry who accepted on behalf of Edmund and agreed to pay all the Pope's expenses into the bargain. Edmund amused himself for a time in distributing the titles and estates of his new kingdom; but by the end of 1257 the whole territory was in the hands of the late Emperor's bastard son, Manfred, and Henry was left with nothing but a huge debt to the papacy and the threat of excommunication if he failed to pay.

Henry turned to the barons and found that they were prepared to help him, but only on condition that he agreed to limit his personal authority, expel his half brothers, and abandon his military ambitions in France. It was a bitter pill to swallow, but he accepted the Provisions of Oxford (1258) which required him to govern with a council of fifteen magnates, sent the Lusignans into exile, and in 1259 signed the Treaty of Paris by which he formally surrendered his claims to Normandy and other French lands. King and barons also acknowledged their responsibility to the wider community. Parliament was to meet three times a year, rather than at the king's whim or not at all; a new justicier was to tour the counties hearing local grievances (the post had been vacant since 1234); and the sheriffs, whose abuse of their office was legendary, were to be local landowners, salaried and appointed for one year only. Other problems, including suit of court (the unpopular obligation to attend a lord's court), and exemption from jury service, were addressed by the Provisions of Westminster in October 1259.

King and barons seemed to have reached an amicable 'constitutional' settlement, but there was a fundamental difference of purpose. Henry believed that if he accepted both Provisions and Treaty the barons would help him conquer Sicily (rather than merely extricate him from his present difficulties), and that his accord with King Louis would permit his forces to march unhindered through France. His willingness to cooperate with the reformers evaporated when he realized that, on the contrary, they were determined to prevent a renewal of the conflict, and he began to undermine the agreement at every opportunity. When de Montfort tried to insist that the Parliament scheduled to meet in February 1260 should not be delayed by the King's absence in France Henry rejected his argument and succeeded in postponing it until after he returned to England. He claimed – disingenuously – that although he was personally committed to the Provisions, the barons' actions in excluding him from government and allegedly allowing his revenues to decline while enriching themselves went far beyond what had been agreed at Oxford, and differences between his opponents (and the temporary absence of some of them from England), allowed him to regain the initiative The justicier's inquiries faltered, the Montfortian sheriffs were replaced by royalists, the Lusignans were restored to favour, and the Pope was persuaded to absolve Henry from his oath to maintain the Provisions in May 1261.

The great weakness of the baronial plan was that, like earlier attempts to restrain other kings, it could only work if the king of the day accepted it. Simon de Montfort and his friends insisted that Henry must be held to his word in all circumstances; but there were other lords who were fundamentally unhappy about the whole business. It was one thing to advise the King – this was something they expected to undertake – but quite another to hold him in thrall and make him do their bidding. They had been brought up to obey the sovereign, to submit to him as the Lord's anointed, and it cut across the grain to insist that he should accept their decisions rather than they his. They chose to believe that Henry would behave more wisely in future – that he would have learned something from his 'short sharp shock' treatment – and that the Provisions would no longer be required.

They were wrong, unfortunately. Henry was still the same old Henry who failed to see trouble coming, and new, arbitrary, demands for money coupled with an uprising in Wales led to protests and to renewed calls for reform. Earl Simon had chosen to go into exile when the King re-asserted his authority (unlike many of his colleagues who had preferred to accept defeat and keep their positions), but returned to demand the restoration of the Provisions in April 1263. He joined forces with the young Earl of Gloucester who Henry had foolishly estranged by refusing to grant him all his late father's properties, and fomented the series of attacks against aliens which a royal clerk later called the 'first war of the barons'. Prince Edward had arrived in England in February bringing with him a large force of foreign mercenaries which could have been used to resist either the Welsh or the resurgent magnates: but his willingness to favour the foreigners at the expense of his English retainers, including, crucially, several powerful landowners from the Welsh marches, only brought more royalists onto de Montfort's side.

Earl Simon and his allies appeared to have regained the initiative, but their position remained vulnerable. They were accused – with some justification – of using their new authority to benefit themselves rather than England, and Edward's disaffected friends soon rejoined him when the foreign soldiers returned home. It was at this point that both sides agreed to submit their differences to the arbitration of Louis IX, a decision for which Simon has been much criticised, but which may not have seemed unreasonable in the circumstances. The Montforts' bond with the French crown, formed when the elder Simon's conquests extended royal authority into the Languedoc earlier in the century, had been carefully nurtured by his son, and Louis had made encouraging noises when the baronial case had been put to him at Boulogne in September. Simon could suppose that a man for whom he had considerable respect and affection would not be indifferent to his cause.

He was badly mistaken, however. Louis was renowned for his fair-mindedness, but he was an absolute monarch dealing with a group of men who, for better or worse, had rebelled against their own king, and gave judgement against them on every point.[8] The Mise of Amiens, as it is known, annulled the Provisions while confirming the King's right to seek the advice of alien counsellors, and the barons had to choose whether to accept both the award and royal autocracy or reject Louis's decision and risk war. Simon made a last, desperate attempt to avoid conflict by offering to accept most of what had been decided at Amiens if Henry would expel the aliens and rule through men committed to England; but the King had confidence in his superior forces and refused to concede anything that would restrict his ability to choose his own advisors. A large number of baronial supporters were captured when the royalists took Northampton on 5 April 1264, but on 14 May Simon defeated Henry at Lewes, in Sussex, and the final, dramatic phase of their relationship began.

Lewes was a great victory won by Simon's superior generalship, but it was not total. Henry and Prince Edward only left the Cluniac priory in which they had taken refuge, and which the Earl dared neither attack nor besiege, after an interim settlement, the 'Mise of Lewes', had been negotiated between them. Henry again accepted the reformers' demands and agreed that baronial prisoners captured at Northampton should be exchanged for royalists taken at Lewes; but Simon had to concede that the Provisions were still negotiable and let several powerful marchers who were bitterly opposed to him go free. It was not an ideal situation, but for the next fifteen months he and two of his principal supporters, the Earl of Gloucester and the Bishop of Chichester, effectively ruled England. They appointed a 'cabinet' of nine to supervise the King and regularly consulted Parliament, a body they sought to make more representative by including knights of the shire on a permanent basis and by summoning burgesses in February 1265. We have previously referred to meetings of the Great Council of the realm as 'parliaments', although the word meant only a 'parleying', an occasion when the king could confer with his notables and discuss matters of state. It was only gradually that men came to distinguish between Council and Parliament, and to see the latter as an independent institution with definite powers and procedures. No one, de Montfort included, would have guessed that these meetings would grow into the central institution of English government; but they had recognized that certain vital aspects of decision-making ought to be consultative and broadly based.

The God of battles had ruled in Earl Simon's favour, but he had crossed the line between reform and rebellion and needed both consent at home and recognition abroad. His direct, personal authority did not extend far beyond his Midlands heartland and London (large areas of England were still in the hands of royalists), and the recent conflict had severely disrupted the regular collection of the Crown's income and allowed local men to settle scores violently without regard to law. There were no further negotiations on the Provisions, mainly because Simon was as reluctant to see them diluted as King Louis was unwilling to sanction treason by varying the Mise of Amiens. Queen Eleanor was in France raising an invasion force that included the Savoyards and Lusignans, and the papal legate added to the barons' difficulties by threatening them with excommunication and the interdict unless they restored Henry to full power.

Simon's government was clearly in some danger, but was rescued by several strokes of good fortune. The legate's authority lapsed when the Pope, Urban IV, died on 2 October (the men of Dover had earlier thrown his bulls [decrees] into the sea to prevent them from being published in England), Queen Eleanor ran out of funds to pay her troops between then and mid-November, and in December the still recalcitrant marchers were defeated and exiled to Ireland for a year and a day. De Montfort could be excused for thinking that the worst of his troubles were now behind him, but the lifting of the threats only allowed differences within the baronial faction to come to the surface. The reformers wanted leadership, but Simon, who could be as abrasive as he was occasionally charming, was never an easy person to deal with, and they resented his apparent readiness to use his position to enrich both himself and his brood of sons. He obliged Prince Edward to give him the earldom of Chester (a move which surely implies that he had no intention of ever allowing Edward to rule independently), and the Earl of Gloucester broke with him because he thought the situation was now little better than when King Henry had ruled arbitrarily and unduly favoured *his* relatives, the Lusignans. Simon had pinned everything on his ability to appeal to as wide a constituency as possible, but their relationship was to be on his terms, not theirs.

There seems little doubt that by the early summer of 1265 Simon's hold over both his party and his kingdom were diminishing, but the real blow was the escape of Prince Edward from custody on 28 May. Edward rapidly came to terms with Gloucester, recruited royalists and the marchers (who had successfully postponed their departure for Ireland), and, after joining forces with William of Lusignan and a group of exiles who had landed in Pembroke, all but cut off his uncle on the wrong side of the Severn. Earl Simon finally crossed the river at Kempsey hoping to link up with another baronial army commanded by his son Simon the younger; but a decisive thrust by Edward defeated these reinforcements at Kenilworth and left his uncle trapped in the loop of the river at Evesham. Here, the dwindling baronial troops were cut to pieces on 4 August, and Earl Simon was killed.

The result was that Henry regained the initiative and was once more free to choose his ministers and councillors: but neither Edward nor Gloucester wanted the achievements of the reform movement to be destroyed. The concept of a limited monarchy had been a temporary expedient to deal with an immediate crisis – even the 1258 reformers had proposed that their arrangement should last only for a twelve year period – but the idea that there must be continuous cooperation between the king and the ruling classes had been firmly implanted in the younger mens' minds. Earl Simon's aims did not die with him, but his rebellion had confounded all attempts to legitimize his position and left him searching for an alternative form of government which did not then exist.

8

THE UNLIKELY SAINT

Simon de Montfort was admired, feared and reviled by his contemporaries in almost equal measure, and subsequent generations have interpreted his actions in similarly black and white terms. Supporters of Charles I and Oliver Cromwell (for example) would have held conflicting opinions of a man who opposed his king in the 'national' interest, and even modern historians have interpreted his career and actions very differently. Professor R.F. Treharne portrayed him as an idealist whose 'moral ascendancy' over his fellow barons made him the leader of the reform movement when their motivation, which was essentially selfish and personal, diminished: but Sir Maurice Powicke saw him as a 'lonely and disconcerting' individual whose rigidity and arrogance contributed to baronial disunity – not a 'constitutionalist born out of his time' but a 'dark force' responsible for distorting and finally destroying the plan of reform. Was he an early upholder of democracy and of freedom from tyranny (a kind of English George Washington), or merely an ambitious rebel baron, and was he really the founder of Parliament? His decision to summon two burgesses from selected boroughs has been seen as a genuine step towards power-sharing, but also as part of a desperate attempt to legitimize his obviously illegal administration. It could also be argued that the rising 'middle classes' were bound to be included in government sooner or later, and he merely anticipated something that would have happened in any event before long.

The struggles between the supporters and the opponents of Henry III exposed several areas of conflict in contemporary society. There were county knights seeking improvements in the law and control of local affairs by local residents; clerics striving to resist royal and papal interference in the Church; and middle elements in the towns struggling to overthrow the ruling oligarchies of rich merchants. They were incidental to the main purpose of the reform movement – the need to place restrictions on an irresponsible and extravagant monarch – but readily identified themselves with it. De Montfort supported the knights when they pressed for the right to choose their own sheriffs, but after Lewes transferred many of their functions to commissioners chosen by and responsible to himself. He was as ready to co-operate with the old ruling oligarchies of townsmen as with their more revolutionary supplanters, and it is particularly interesting that he proposed summoning only barons and prelates to the parliament he planned for June 1265. It was left to his sometime enemy Prince Edward, when he became king, to make the inclusion of knights and burgesses a regular feature of political life in England, and to do what Earl Simon might not have done had he lived. Overall, Simon appears to have been more concerned to concentrate power in his own hands than to devolve it upon others, and more than ready to cooperate with those in authority (in the interests of stability), whether he approved of their politics or not.

We cannot seek to peer into the mind and fully understand the motivations of a man who lived seven centuries ago, but there is no doubting de Montfort's energy, his fearlessness, his versatility and his piety, the qualities his contemporaries admired. He was equally at home planning a campaign, governing a province or kingdom, or conversing on equal terms with churchmen, and it is still somewhat remarkable that such a talented individual should have died in such appalling circumstances. We must never forget that he was first and foremost a man of his time, a great lord wedded to the existing social order. His rebellion was not a revolution that sought to give 'power to the people', but was founded on the premise that only he – and not the King – could give England the good government the country needed. He would probably not have appreciated the irony that he was an alien who resented and expelled aliens, or that the fact that his sons were as much King John's grandsons as Henry's might lead some to suspect that he was seeking the crown for his own family. His mind was fixed on higher things.

Simon's impact upon his contemporaries can be explained only in terms of his dominant personality, but this also contained the seeds of his undoing in that he lacked the tact needed to handle the complex personal relationships that constituted so much of the politics of his day. His greatest friends and most devoted supporters were clergymen – men like the Franciscan friar Adam Marsh and the bishops Robert Grosseteste of Lincoln and Walter Cantilupe of Worcester who saw him as a devout Christian who shared their values – and it is part of his tragedy that politics and ambition soured his relationships with secular figures. Dr Knowles's assessment is that:

> Simon's career is less of a puzzle if we abandon the view that the
> self-seeking adventurer of the 1230s evolved into an enlightened

altruistic reformer thirty years later. In fact, his temper remained remarkably consistent and recalls both his fanatical father and his turbulent sons. Simon's preoccupation with personal advancement; his complete confidence in his own uprightness, his capacity for violence; his exasperation with, and domineering attitude towards, the king; his deference to clerics, the only people able to influence him: these characteristics recur throughout his career. It was not Simon so much as the times that changed.[1]

But change the times did, and de Montfort, uncompromising, and committed to a cause which, in the last resort, was as illegal as it was unacceptable, paid the ultimate price.

Simon de Montfort was dead and that was the end of the matter, or at least, that is what King Henry and Prince Edward would have supposed. But they could not have been more mistaken. On 7 August 1265, only three days after Evesham, a group of royalists led by Eudo la Zuche, one of the King's standard bearers, and Peter de Nevil, marshal of the Household, rode into the village of Peatling Magna in south Leicestershire. They were followed, a day later, by one of de Nevil's grooms, bringing a cart with supplies, 'and some foolish men of the village, seeking to arrest the cart and horses', wounded him in the arm above his hand.[2] Peter retaliated by threatening to burn the village when he returned on the 12th, and after negotiations it was agreed that a fine of twenty marks – a large sum for a small community – should be paid to him the following Sunday. Hostages were demanded, and five freeholders surrendered as sureties; but the money was not forthcoming and they languished in prison until early the following January. The reeve, priest and others denied promising to pay de Nevil when the matter came to court in November 1266, but the jurors found against them and ordered them to settle. They were also told to give a mark to each of the five hostages for allowing them to be incarcerated for so long.

All this would doubtless be regarded as a minor, local incident of only passing interest but for one remarkable fact. When Peter returned to Peatling Magna on 12 August, the villagers told him not only that he was unwelcome, but that he and his men were guilty of sedition and 'other heinous offences'. He was, they said' 'going against the welfare of the community of the realm, and against the barons'. We do not know precisely what they meant by the 'community of the realm', or how or why the concept concerned them as individuals. But they clearly thought that de Montfort and his baronial supporters were an essential part of it, and that those who had slain him were neither their friends nor friends of England. Earl Simon was not just another overlord who had lost his life in a dispute with his peers that was of no interest to the average peasant: here was something that mattered and something worth fighting for.

These sentiments were not confined to Peatling Magna or to people who lived in Earl Simon's titular county. A lament composed soon after his death at Evesham was clearly written for all those who admired him and regretted his loss:

> I must sing, my heart wishes it, in a grievous strain; in tears was
> made the song of our gentle baronage, who for the sake of peace so
> long deferred, let themselves be torn asunder, their bodies hacked
> and dismembered to save England. (Refrain). 'Now he is slain, the
> flower of fame, who was so versed in warfare, Montfort the earl;
> the whole land bewailed his cruel death.'[3]

Some of this is exaggerated, but must still represent popular opinion. The same is true of verse three:

> But by his death earl Montfort won the victory; like the martyr of Canterbury he ended his life. The good Thomas did not want holy church to be destroyed; the earl also fought and died without flinching. Now he is slain, etc.

Archbishop Thomas Becket, who had been canonized in just a little over two years after his murder in Canterbury Cathedral in December 1170, had become one of the most revered saints in western Christendom, and it is remarkable that the composer of the lament should compare him with de Montfort. They had both died opposing a king named Henry, both had antagonized many of their contemporaries, and both were to some extent victims of their own stubbornness; but in reality few outside Earl Simon's circle of admirers would have spoken of them in the same breath. Yet there is more. Verse six continues:

> Near his body, that great treasure, they found a hair shirt. The false knaves, they were so wicked, and those who killed him. It was worse that they had the good man dismembered, who knew so well all there was to know about fighting and keeping faith. Now he is slain etc.

Becket had been very much a man of the world when he had served Henry II as chancellor, and had become deeply aesthetic only after being appointed archbishop. There were some who thought that he was acting a part rather than fulfilling a genuine vocation; but all this changed when the monks who prepared his body for burial found that he had been wearing a hair shirt next to his skin. No play-actor would have worn such a garment – the lice infesting it would have caused him untold suffering – and, deeply impressed, 'they prostrated themselves on the ground, kissed his hands and feet, and invoked him as St Thomas'.[4] They would not have done so if he had been dressed in 'underclothes of samite and silk', to quote Professor Barlow,[5] and the writer of the song wanted to prove that de Montfort was similarly 'righteous' and deserving of admiration. He says only that a hair shirt was found near the Earl's body (not that he was actually wearing it), but there seems little doubt that the austerely religious Simon did wear such a garment on occasion and may well have done so in the expectation that his battle at Evesham would be his last.

The authorities doubtless hoped that such sentiments would die a natural death after a short period, but by the time the Dictum of Kenilworth was drawn up in September and October 1267 they were becoming seriously concerned. The *Dictum* was the work of a committee of twelve (eight barons and four bishops), charged with devising a process whereby those who had forfeited their lands for supporting the rebellion could recover them on terms. The 'disinherited' were fined twice, five times, or (in a few cases) seven times the annual value of their properties according to the seriousness of their offences, and required to submit to the King's peace within forty days. Among other things, they had to pay compensation for 'improvements' made to their estates while they had been in the hands of others, and were forbidden to say or do anything that would enhance Earl Simon's reputation. Article 8 was framed as follows:

Humbly asking both the lord legate and the lord king that he, the lord legate, should absolutely forbid on pain of ecclesiastical punishment Simon earl of Leicester to be regarded by anyone as a saint or a just man, since he died excommunicate as holy church holds. And the vain and fatuous marvels told of him by some, ever to be uttered by any lips [i.e. are not to be repeated]. And that the lord king be pleased strictly to forbid these same things on pain of bodily punishment.[6]

The legate's sentence of excommunication had been published at Hesdin in Flanders after the physical destruction of the bulls bound for England at Dover, so how could a ruthless baron who was under the Church's anathema become a saint? The answer is that his canonization had nothing to do with the Church but was informal and popular. The monks of Evesham had given his dismembered remains honourable burial after the battle, and by the time the *Dictum* was formulated his grave had become a place of pilgrimage. Even the pool of water on Green Hill near where he had fallen was believed to have healing properties, and became the site of a stone chapel built for the benefit of those who came to be cured of their ills.

An individual's saintliness is confirmed by the miracles he or she is believed to work, and in Simon's case this was no small number. One of the monks recorded over 200 of them,[7] some effected by keeping vigil, others by drinking or washing in water from the pool (the 'Earl's well', as it came to be known), or by rubbing dust taken from his tomb into the affected area. Those too ill to travel to Evesham in person could bend a penny in Simon's name (to 'mark' the particular coin being offered), or have their body or diseased limb 'measured' with a thread which was then incorporated into a candle lit in the Earl's honour. A few examples will give the flavour of them:

A certain man of Hawkesbury, dumb and convulsed for seven years, being measured by the Earl immediately recovered from his infirmities. The Abbot of Pershore testifies to this.

Avicia, daughter of Alan of Derby, after being unquestionably dead, roused herself and got well on being measured by Earl Simon.

William, surnamed Child, had a son who was sick to death, at which William was sore grieved. By chance a certain friar preacher, an old companion of his, came to him, and seeing his grief, asked if he had ever been at enmity with Earl Simon. And he said, 'Yes, for he deprived me of my goods.' And the other answered, 'Ask pardon of the martyr, and thou shalt recover thy child.' Meanwhile the child died, and the father in great grief threw himself upon his bed and slept. And he saw in a dream Christ descend from heaven and touch him, saying, 'Whatever thou asketh in the name of my Earl shall be given thee'. And he rose in haste and measured the boy, and he opened his eyes. Of this Clement of London and the father of the dead boy are witnesses.

The Earl who took William's goods sounds much more like the real de Montfort, and he was still a dangerous man to cross:

Philip, chaplain of Brentley, reviled the Earl and said, 'If the Earl be a saint, as they say, may the devil break my neck or some miracle happen before I come home.' And as he asked so it came to pass. For in returning home he saw a hare, and pursuing it, fell from his horse. Of this the whole city of Hereford bear witness.

A similar incident took place at Bolney, in Sussex, about eighteen months after the battle, when a William de la Horste was entertaining some guests who criticised Earl Simon. William stood up for his hero, and may have felt vindicated when one of the critics suffered a stroke! Anyone, from the greatest to the least, could appeal to him, and even animals were not beneath his notice.

> Gregory de Grandun, rector of Sapcote, reports that 'his ox would not eat for fifteen days, but immediately recovered on a coin being bent in honour of Simon'.

> The Countess of Gloucester had a palfrey which had been broken-winded for two years. When at Evesham the horse drank at the Earl's well, and having had its head and face washed with the water recovered. The Countess and all her company are witnesses.

Christ had changed water into wine, but Earl Simon changed water into beer and back again!

> A sick woman of Elmley sent her daughter to the Earl's well to fetch water. In returning she met the servants of the castle, who asked her what she had in the pitcher. She answered that it was new beer from Evesham, and they said, 'Nay, but it is water from the Earl's well.' But when they had drawn some forth, they found it as the girl had said, and so they let her go. And when she came to the sick woman it was again changed into water, and the sick woman having drunk thereof, was healed.[8]

We cannot, at this distance in time, fathom the extent to which these people were deluding themselves or being deluded, but they believed that miracles could, and sometimes did, happen. Earl

Simon was credited with the ability to work them, and some of his aura even rubbed off on his companions. His son Henry and his close friend Hugh le Despenser, who were buried near him in the abbey, also had cures attributed to them, and he remained closely associated with Bishop Robert Grosseteste of Lincoln who had been his principal confidant until his death in 1253. Grosseteste was a saintly man who might have been canonized in other circumstances and who could be expected to work miracles on his own account, but there are strong indications that people appealed to him at least partly because he reminded them of the Earl and his cause:

A certain young man around sixteen years old, being taken by his father and mother to Robert, the holy bishop of Lincoln, and coming there with his father and mother, on Saturday next before the battle that took place on the Tuesday at Evesham, began to sleep; and he continued to sleep in that dormitory through the whole night, and until the first hour of the Monday next following. Who then waking up, began to speak, even though he had been mute for the whole time of his life, saying to his father and mother: 'Why are you waiting here?' They answered: 'On account of your salvation that is to be obtained from St Robert the bishop.' He said to them: 'The said holy bishop is not here, for he has gone to Evesham to the aid of earl Simon, his brother, who is to die at Evesham on the Tuesday next following.' And thus the aforesaid youth, previously mute, convalesced, who, bearing witness to these things, still lives in the church of Lincoln.[9]

But why was Earl Simon, who had been the implacable opponent of the King and a section of the baronage, held in such high regard by ordinary people? The answer is almost certainly that they regarded him as a 'leader of the opposition', and thought that their generally hard lot in life would have become somehow easier if his government had lasted. They were deceiving themselves of course. Simon was an aristocrat and his dispute was with his royal brother-in-law and other members of the aristocracy. We have noted that he had no concept of a society in which peasants had a say in how they were governed, and that even his most famous decision – to summon knights and burgesses to the February 1265 Parliament – was not inspired by a commitment to greater democracy. He wanted the rising middle classes to support his illegal government, but sharing power with them, amending policies to accommodate their wishes, was never part of his agenda. Many who idolized him would have become disillusioned when he failed to fulfil their expectations, and it is perhaps fortunate – in one sense – that he died before this could happen. They could continue to believe that he would have changed society for the better, and his reputation remained intact.

It is not easy to determine how long Earl Simon's cult lasted. A least 135 'miracles' were recorded in 1265–6, but there were fewer than thirteen in 1267–8 when the threats made in the *Dictum* probably dissuaded many from visiting the tomb or reporting their 'cures'. It picked up a little after this, perhaps when the authorities became less vigilant, but ended shortly before, or soon after, 1280.[10] At some point, again probably in response to the *Dictum*, Simon's body was moved to a more obscure and unconsecrated part of the abbey. The Annals of Osney record that his remains were 'exhumed, and thrown down in some remote spot; which place is, to this day, hidden and unknown, except to very few people',[11] and the government may have felt that it had dealt prudently with what had once seemed a serious threat. It was not quite the end, however. When Edward II stayed at Whorlton Castle in Yorkshire in September 1322, he was entertained by two local women, Agnes the Redhaired and Alice of Whorlton, who sang songs of Simon de Montfort.[12] The King may have had mixed feelings about the man who had so troubled his father and grandfather, but he was sufficiently impressed by the performance to give Agnes and Alice the generous sum of four shillings. He was less accommodating when, two years later, he complained in a letter that people continued to venerate Simon, and that bogus miracles were being worked at a gibbet in Bristol where the dry bones of some of his followers still hung in chains. He suspected that enemies were seeking to turn memories of the Earl to their own advantage, whipping up animosity against him on account of his royal blood. Clearly, Simon's was still a name to conjure with almost sixty years after his death.

To make matters worse, Edward had a popular martyr of his own to deal with in the aftermath of Earl Thomas of Lancaster's rebellion in 1322. Within six weeks of Lancaster's execution there were reports of miracles being worked at the Pontefract church where his body rested, and next year a mob allegedly 2,000 strong killed two of the constable's servants who were attempting to prevent people making offerings on the small hill outside the castle where he had been beheaded:

Commission to Henry le Scrop, John de Doncastr' and John de Denum. Barnard Castle, 9 September 17 Edward II [1323].

The king formerly commanded Richard de Moseleye, his clerk, constable of Pontefract castle, to go in person to the place of execution of Thomas, late earl of Lancaster, and prohibit a multitude of malefactors and apostates from praying and making oblations there in memory of the said earl, not to God but rather to idols, in contempt of the king and contrary to his former command. The said constable and his servants were assaulted at Pontefract, and two of them named Richard de Godeleye and Robert de la Hawe were killed.

The commissioners are to inquire into this and imprison such persons as should be indicted before them.[13]

But it made little difference. Local people christened the place St Thomas's hill, and a chapel was built for the benefit of pilgrims. A hagiographical 'life' appeared in the fifteenth century, and his hat and belt, which were said to cure headaches and to assist in childbirth, were preserved at Pontefract until the Reformation. The problem would not go away.

Earl Thomas, like Earl Simon before him, had seemed to offer an alternative to the rule of a harsh yet ineffective government, and his posthumous popularity can only be explained in these terms. His cult certainly overshadowed de Montfort's, and may even have replaced it. There are no more references to Simon's after the 1320s, and a new generation may have felt that they had more in common with Lancaster than with someone admired by their grandparents. The older associations still lingered, however. In South Newington Church in Oxfordshire is a wall painting showing Earl Thomas kneeling, blood spurting from a gash in his neck, awaiting a second blow from the executioner; and nearby, watching, is St Thomas of Canterbury – Thomas Becket![14]

9

THE DISINHERITED

Henry III was in no small measure responsible for the civil war, and was equally guilty of failing to pacify the country in its aftermath. De Montfort's death at Evesham was followed by a free-for-all in which royalists seized lands from baronial sympathizers, a situation the King did nothing to improve when he announced that he would take all the rebels' estates into his own hands to dispose of as he thought fit. The result was that men who had nothing to lose saw no reason to abandon the struggle as they might have done if reasonable terms had been offered them, and the conflict dragged on long after it should have been brought to an end.

The situation that was allowed to develop after August 1265 was unfair in several ways. Some royalist supporters fared better than others – those who seized most land were not necessarily those who had contributed most to the royal victory – while some 'rebels' whose properties were seized by more powerful local rivals had never been wedded to the Earl's cause. Some of those who stole lands – as well as some who continued to resist the government – were probably no more than brigands or freebooters taking advantage of the dislocation caused by the war and the lack of a strong central authority. Such opportunities came but seldom and were not to be missed.

Those most severely affected were inevitably the surviving members of Earl Simon's family. The Countess Eleanor (the King's sister), sent her younger sons to France when she heard of her husband's death, and crossed the Channel with her daughter Eleanor on 28 October, never to return. Henry, her eldest son, had been slain with his father at Evesham, and of the others, Guy (who had been wounded), and Simon the younger, joined her in exile in the early months of 1266. The earldom of Leicester had already been bestowed on the King's younger son, Edmund (it was not Sicily but it was something), and it was clear that none of the de Montforts had any future in England. Simon and Guy subsequently had chequered careers as mercenaries in the pay of King Louis's brother, Charles of Anjou, but another of their brothers, Amaury, became a noted scholar. The empty titles he took to himself – by hereditary right Earl of Leicester and Chester and steward of England – speak eloquently of how much they had lost.

But what of those for whom flight abroad was not an option? A number of them were surprised at Chesterfield of 15 May 1266, but the defeat did not lead to the surrender of their strongholds at Kenilworth and the Isle of Ely. Kenilworth was besieged for several months until the royalists wearied of their task, and it was only then that the King relented and allowed the new papal legate, Cardinal Ottobuono Fieschi, to promote the compromise which culminated in the Dictum of Kenilworth. We noted in the last chapter how the Dictum permitted offenders to recover their estates on payment of a fine fixed at between two and seven times the annual value;[1] but how was an individual's culpability to be assessed, and who could be sure that the same criteria were being applied evenly across the country? There were bound to be those who thought that they had been treated harshly while others had escaped relatively lightly, and saw no reason to accept a 'solution' which (in their opinion), discriminated against them. The dispute would go on.

The defenders of Kenilworth hoped that forces Simon the Younger was recruiting in France would arrive to relieve them, but when none appeared they surrendered on 14 December. An attack on Ely was delayed while attempts were made to persuade the rebels there to do likewise, but the situation changed dramatically when the Earl of Gloucester decided to march on London at the beginning of April 1267. Gloucester had been disappointed with the rewards he had received after Evesham – others, like the leading marcher lord Roger Mortimer, had fared much better – and had no intention of allowing his rivals to effectively steal his victory. He was joined in the capital by John d'Eyvill, the leader of the Ely garrison, and together they fortified Southwark, cut off access from the Tower, and dug a ditch around the walls. Prince Edward was away restoring order in Northumberland, and on hearing the news hurried southwards gathering men and provisions in anticipation of a siege. The process of reconciliation looked about to unravel, but was saved by negotiations and by a general reluctance to provoke more conflict. Gloucester promised to keep the peace and was reconciled with Edward, while d'Eyvill and his followers were granted immediate possession of their lands and were helped to meet the fines imposed on them. A few dissidents continued to hold out in Ely, but Edward defeated them later in the year.

The surrender of Kenilworth, Ely and Southwark deprived the Montfortians of their three main centres of resistance, but there were still individuals and small bands of outlaws who continued to cause trouble. One of these was Roger Godberd whose career will be discussed in detail in the next chapter, but another was

Adam Gurdon who established himself near the notorious pass at Alton and lived by plunder and highway robbery. Again, it was Prince Edward who finally forced him into submission, and who then gave him land in Alton instead of punishing him. There is nothing to substantiate Nicholas Trivet's story that Gurdon won Edward's respect after the two of them engaged in personal combat; but Edward knew a good man when he saw one, and we may agree with Professor Pollard that 'there are enough echoes here to make one wonder whether the story did not find its way into the *Gest*'.[2]

Wars always produce winners and losers, and this one was no exception. Most former rebels recovered the majority of their properties, but the sums they paid for the privilege resulted in a considerable re-distribution of wealth. John d'Eyvill had been treated relatively leniently, but he was already in debt to Jewish moneylenders and could not meet his obligations to them *and* pay his fine. The King allowed him to defer payment of the sums owed to Jews while he redeemed his lands, but more than half his fine remained outstanding in November 1272 and he did not begin to repay his earlier debts until at least 1275. On the other hand, the royalist Walter de Merton, who had been chancellor in 1261–3, did very well for himself. He had created a foundation for the support of scholars studying at Oxford, and took advantage of the post-war situation to enrich it by acquiring the estates of several insolvent Montfortians, usually by discharging their debts to the Jews in return. Merton College, Oxford, is the fruit of his work.[3]

The extent of the royalists' gains and the rebels' losses inevitably varied, and it is a curious irony that two contrasting individuals – a rebel who suffered particularly badly and a royalist who was one of the principal beneficiaries – are both central to our story.

The 'loser' was Robert de Ferrers, Earl of Derby, described by Dr Maddicott as the 'wild card' among the barons.[4] Ferrers was a young man who only joined the reform movement after he came of age in 1260, and whose opposition to the Crown owed more to his personal differences with Prince Edward than to matters of principle. He particularly coveted the Peveril inheritance which his grandfather had been obliged to surrender in 1222 and which had been given to Edward in 1254, and the situation was not improved when Edward attacked and devastated his lands in Derbyshire and Staffordshire before Lewes. Edward's imprisonment after the battle allowed Ferrers to repay the compliment by seizing Peveril Castle from its royal custodian and by attacking Chester, but this brought him into direct conflict with Earl Simon when Simon appointed himself lord of Chester and the Peak in December. Summoned to London to attend the February 1265 parliament, he was confined to the Tower, and was still languishing there in August when Simon's government came to a bloody end.

Ferrers's lack of commitment to the baronial cause should have stood him in good stead with the royalist victors of Evesham, and he was indeed pardoned in December on payment of 1,500 marks and a gold cup. But nothing had been done to resolve his differences with Edward, and he was among the Montfortians defeated and captured at Chesterfield in May 1266. His lands were given to the King's son Edmund shortly after he was imprisoned at Windsor, and his redemption fine under the terms of the Dictum of Kenilworth was fixed at the maximum seven times their annual value. The 'disinherited' did not normally have to find the money in advance – usually, they were reinstated immediately and allowed to pay in instalments – but Ferrers was treated particularly harshly. Edmund was ordered to restore his lands to him on 1 May 1269, but on the same day forced him to sign an agreement which required him to pay £50,000 (a fine far in excess of seven times his yearly income),[5] to redeem his estates and secure his freedom. He had no hope of finding, or even borrowing, such a huge amount either then or at any time thereafter, and although he was released from prison ceased to be Earl of Derby in anything but name. In 1274 he brought an action against Edmund pleading that he had signed under duress 'in fear of his life' and should be allowed to recover his lands according to the strict terms of the Dictum; but Edmund successfully argued that their private arrangement superseded the Dictum and that Ferrers had sealed it as a legally binding deed.[6] Ferrers's real problem was that his feud with Edward had soured his relations with the royal family, while the Montfortians regarded him as at best a perfidious ally. He was either unpopular or treated with suspicion, and had few friends in his hour of need.

On the other side of the divide stood a man called Roger Leyburn who was as highly regarded as Ferrers was despised. Leyburn, the son of a Kentish knight, was born about 1220 although little is known of him for the first thirty years of his life. In 1252 he killed one of the King's household knights, Arnulf de Munteny, in a tournament (Matthew Paris says he deliberately used a sharpened lance because Arnulf had injured him in a previous combat), but he soon regained royal favour and became closely associated with Prince Edward. He campaigned with Edward in Wales, and served him as bailiff of his lands until he was accused of embezzling the proceeds of the manor of Elham (Kent), in 1262.[7] This caused him to throw in his lot with the marchers (who were opposing the King at this point in the conflict), and to actively co-operate with Earl Simon; but his flirtation with the barons was only temporary and he had rejoined the royalists by August 1263. His *volte-face* was remarkable even in that age of shifting alliances, and Gervase of Canterbury was moved to comment that 'Saul became Paul and the wolf was made a lamb'.[8]

We do not know if the rewards Leyburn subsequently received – steward of the King's household, warden of the Cinque Ports, and Sheriff of Kent – had been offered to him before he changed sides, but there can be no doubt that his abilities were highly regarded. He was with King Henry at Northampton, fought for him again at Lewes, and helped to sustain the royalist cause in Wales during the period of baronial government. His opposition to Earl Simon cost him his wardenship, but his allegiance never wavered and he was among those who masterminded Edward's escape from custody in May 1265. He was again present on the royal side at Evesham, and was credited with rescuing the captive King from the melee in which de Montfort and his leading supporters were killed.

Leyburn's support had been crucial to the eventual triumph of the royalist party, and he benefited accordingly. Henry granted him rebel estates in his native Kent and other counties, and his numerous appointments included the constableship of Carlisle and Nottingham castles and the shirevealty of Cumberland. He became a member of the royal council, and in September 1266 the King required his lieges 'to do his knight, Sir Roger Leyburn, special favour on account of his many services'... and asked that 'all persons receive him everywhere with due honour as the king's knight'.[9] Campaigns against London (which still adhered to the Montfortians) and rebels in the Weald and in Essex were punctuated by successful attacks on Sandwich and Winchelsea, but he was unable to prevent John d'Eyvill from joining the Earl of Gloucester in London in April 1267. Henry instructed him to cross to France to secure the services of the Counts of St Pol and Boulogne for the impending conflict, and their presence in the royal army may have helped to facilitate a peaceful outcome. So many tasks meant that he had to rely upon deputies to fulfil most of his offices, and the same must have been true of the commission he received on 29 July to pacify the disinherited in Nottingham, Derby, Lancaster, York, Northumberland, Cumberland and Westmorland. It was his deputy at Nottingham, Alan de Kirby, reinforced by Leyburn's son, William, who defeated a group of local rebels in Charnwood Forest (Leicestershire) on 14 September.

The gradual normalization of the situation in England allowed Leyburn to turn his attention to other matters, and in August 1269 he joined Prince Edward and King Louis in making plans for a new crusade. He accompanied the expedition which sailed from Dover a year later, but returned to England within three months and died, probably in October 1271. Robert de Ferrers lived until 1279 and recovered two of his former manors in the early years of Edward I's reign, but he was never again a figure of consequence. After his death his widow (his second wife, who he had married after his fall from grace), sued Edmund 'Crouchback' for a dower third of his former holdings. Edmund resisted her claim of the grounds that Ferrers had not been seized of the lands when he married her or at any time thereafter, but gave her the manor of Godmanchester for her lifetime in 1281. It is a curious comment on the complex matrimonial relationships of the period that Robert de Ferrers's mother, Margaret, was the daughter of Roger de Quincy, Earl of Winchester (the possessor of the 'other' half of the Leicester inheritance), while de Quincy's second wife, Eleanor, who was herself a Ferrers, married Roger Leyburn after his death![10]

Henry III's death and Prince Edward's accession as Edward I in 1272 fundamentally altered the situation, not least because the new King was a man of proven ability who enjoyed the confidence of his principal subjects. Edward had fostered the process of reconciliation, partly, perhaps, because he wanted to put the troubles of the past decade behind him, but equally because he had little practical alternative. The ruler of a small country with a limited number of fighting men and local administrators could not tolerate a situation in which a significant part of the body politic was permanently alienated from him, and it was inevitable that the majority of those who had supported or fought with Earl Simon would be reconciled and restored to office. Dr Knowles has estimated that when Edward began to prepare for his invasion of Wales in 1276, one in ten of the earls, barons and knights summoned had been in arms against him ten years earlier.[11] He gives several examples of former rebels who regained royal favour, notably Ralph of Sandwich, who may have been a brother of Henry of Sandwich, the pro-Montfortian Bishop of London, and John de Vescy, who had been one of Earl Simon's principal northern backers. Both were captured at Evesham, and de Vescy rebelled again in 1267; but Ralph became a steward of the King's demesnes and subsequently constable of the Tower of London, while John accompanied Edward on crusade and became one of his closest friends. Only the most intractable – or unlucky – of rebels failed to find a way back.

ROGER GODBERD & WALTER DEVYAS

We know something of the careers and the troubles experienced by Earl Simon's greatest supporters, but there were many others whose lives were disrupted to a greater or lesser extent. A retainer, or a tenant, could plead that he had followed his lord into opposition to the Crown because he had no practical alternative, an argument that would probably be accepted if he was genuinely contrite and seemed likely to behave himself in future. It is impossible to tell how many of those who sided with the baronial party did so because they were morally certain that they were pursuing the right course of action; but the fact that some lesser men who might have made their peace continued to resist the King after Evesham would suggest that they were not all time-servers or reluctant combatants. They remained loyal to the ideal even when the going became difficult and there was little prospect of success.

Such a man was Roger Godberd, a tenant of Robert de Ferrers, Earl of Derby, who held land at Swannington in north-west Leicestershire. Not much is known of the Godberds – they seem to have named most of their eldest sons 'Roger' and to have been ever on the look-out for opportunities[1] – and it was only the events of the thirteenth century that brought them to wider notice. 'Our'

Roger was probably born at the beginning of the 1230s and died in the early 1290s at a little over sixty years of age. His father's early death allowed his mother, Margaret, and her second husband, Anketil de Swaninton (sic), to take possession of a dower third of the family's holdings, and at Easter 1250 Roger protested that they had wasted his inheritance by cutting down and selling sixty oak trees worth 100 shillings. An inquiry subsequently found in Margaret and Anketil's favour, and it was only Roger's age (he was still under twenty-one) that saved him from being fined for making false accusations.[2] It was not an auspicious beginning, but here was someone who, although still a teenager, was clearly prepared to stand up for himself.

Roger had at least two brothers, William and Geoffrey, and was married, although his wife's name is not recorded. They were clearly on good terms with the Thringstone family who came from the neighbouring village of the same name, and it is possible that Roger himself married a Thringstone just as his son was to do years later. Both feature in the surviving Hastings papers (Ashby de la Zouch, the Hastings family seat, is only a stone's throw from both Swannington and Thringstone), where it is noted that 'Huelyna, daughter of Robert de Threngeston [Thringstone], married Roger Godbert [the younger] of Swannington'. Robert's son William generously gave them some land in Thringstone with the proviso that it revert to the grantor if Huelyna died without having children. Roger himself witnessed a deed on behalf of the Thringstones, and Robert's widow quitclaimed some land to him, both at unknown dates.[3]

Roger had at least two children, the Roger noticed above who succeeded him and who was still living in 1306,[4] and a daughter named Diva. Diva is mentioned in a volume entitled *Excerpta è*

Rotulis Finium in Turri Londinensi asservatis, Henrico tertio rege,
II, 1247–72 where it is recorded that in 42 Henry III (1258):

> Leyc' Diva filia Rogi de Godeberd' dat dimid marca p una assis no
> dis.cap. coram Gilbto de Preston. Et mand est Vic Leyc' qd cap tc'
> (Leicestershire. Diva daughter of Roger de Godeberd' gives half a
> mark for an assize of novel disseisin to be taken before Gilbert de
> Preston. And the sheriff of Leicester[shire] is instructed to take...)[5]

The entry is a puzzle inasmuch as it does not say what the sheriff is to take – steps to arrange the assize presumably – nor does it indicate what the case was about. An assize of novel disseisin ('recent dispossession') was an action to recover lands of which the plaintiff had been disseised, or dispossessed, but Diva is unlikely to have held property unless she had been married and widowed. The implication is that she had been wedded at an early age (her father was still under thirty), but that her husband had died leaving her with a dower third of his estate and perhaps other lands which his family had settled on them in jointure. Her in-laws would have been reluctant to see a significant part of what they still considered to be 'their' property alienated to a young widow for what might prove to be a long lifetime, and they had presumably tried to recover it forcibly. The assize did not deal with the issue of lawful possession. It simply asked whether a dispossession had taken place in which case the property was restored to the plaintiff until the question of rightful ownership could be dealt with. We do not know how Diva fared, unfortunately, and her name is never mentioned again.

Roger Godberd is unlikely to have played any part in the troubles of the late 1250s since his lord, Robert de Ferrers, did not come of age until 1260, and the next time we hear of him is in 1260 when he was involved in another dispute over land. He had leased Swannington manor to a Jordan le Fleming for ten years, but within twelve months had forcibly ejected him from the property misappropriating chattels worth £20 in the process.[6] Roger did not appear in court to answer Jordan's complaint, and was clearly prepared to act illegally (hoping to take advantage of the central government's weakness), and to recruit others in order to resort to violence. It was a foretaste of things to come.

We do not know precisely why Roger decided to allow another man to farm his principal manor, but at some point in the late 1250s or early 1260s he became a member of the garrison of Nottingham Castle. It may be that his new military responsibilities and frequent absences from home initially made running an estate impractical (or at least that was what he had supposed when he leased Swannington), but that he subsequently found that he had more time on his hands than he had expected and wanted the manor back! On 18 December 1264 Roger was one of a total of forty-one members of the garrison (including John Grey, the former constable, and his son Reginald), who were granted protection until the following Easter. He received 'safe conduct for him and his household in going to his lands, staying there and going thence whither he will' on condition that 'he will stand his trial in the king's court if any will proceed against him touching any trespasses'.[7] We could assume that this had something to do with his dispute with Fleming, but the number of others involved suggests that it related principally to the battle of Lewes, fought seven months earlier. They had probably joined the King (or at least failed to answer de Montfort's summons), and needed to tread carefully now that baronial supporters were in charge.[8]

The treatment of royalists, and even 'neutrals', presented the new government with a serious problem. Earl Simon had fought against the King and captured him, but he had not deposed him even though he now ruled in his name. Enemies could not accuse one another of treason when they all recognised the same monarch, and none of them wanted more conflict. Godberd and his companions were too numerous – and collectively too powerful – to be excluded or forced into permanent opposition, and the Montfortian regime accepted that it could only build on its victory if they, and others like them, accepted the situation. Reconciliation would have to come sooner or later, and the 'protection' granted to the castle garrison may have been a step in this process. They were not to be harried, and all would eventually be well.

There is no evidence that Godberd was at Evesham (Ferrers, his lord, was still a prisoner in the Tower of London), but he is likely to have been among the rebels surprised and defeated at Chesterfield on 15 May 1266. The Earl of Derby's differences with Prince Edward had again come to a head after he regained his freedom, and he brought both himself and his followers to the 'baronial', or, more precisely, anti-royalist, side of the argument. Godberd evaded capture (unlike his unfortunate master), but remained in arms and behaved in a generally lawless manner. He had previously leased land and incurred debts to the monks of Garendon (Leicestershire), and in September and October appeared before the abbey with a gang of brigands and compelled the fearful brethren to return everything to him. The *Close Roll* records that:

Roger Godeberd of Swaneton came at Gerewedon [Garendon] and took and carried away by extortion the charters, which he had made to the abbot and convent of Gerewedon concerning one assart [a piece of land converted from forest to arable] and a wood in the same town and concerning a quittance of 5s. and certain land, which they held of the same man for a term, and one deed obligatory of seven marks, in which he was bound to them, on Saturday next after the feast of the Nativity of the Blessed Mary in the 50th year of the reign of the king [1266]. In the same year on the day of St Calixtus next following [14 October] the same Roger caused the said abbot and convent by force and compulsion to make him a certain charter of quittance concerning all the things, above-said.[9]

In spite of this, on 14 November Godberd, Roger de Remes, Nicholas de la Hus' and three others were granted safe conduct to come to Court within the next eight days 'to treat of peace for themselves and those in their company'. The majority did so (Roger de Remes was admitted to the peace and pardoned on 25 November), but Godberd failed to appear and was given a further period of grace to last until the Sunday after the feast of St Andrew the Apostle (30 November). It is unclear if he was still reluctant to submit or whether he had been prevented from attending by circumstances, but he and his brother William were both pardoned on 10 December.[10] Rehabilitation came at a price, however:

Admission to the king's peace of Roger Godbert and William his brother; and pardon to them of all their trespasses and forfeitures in the time of the late disturbance on condition of their good behaviour: and grant to them that the lands which they now hold shall not incur loss thereby provided that they stand to the award of Kenilworth *with regard to their lands which the king has given to others* [my italics]. And if they offend against their fealty again, their bodies shall be at the king's will, and their lands shall fall (*incurrantur*) to the king and his heirs forever.[11]

Like others, the Godberds would have been able to recover their lands almost immediately, but their finances would have been severely straightened for some time.

Roger effectively disappears from the record for between three and four years after 1266, and his activities have been the subject of some speculation. He may have lived quietly, farming and perhaps selling timber to pay off his debts, but it is curious that a group of Nottinghamshire rebels who continued to resist the authorities found refuge in his backyard in Charnwood Forest. Roger Leyburn, whose career we discussed in the last chapter, was one of those charged with defeating them, and sent his son William with a company of eight knights and twenty 'serjeants' (literally, 'common soldiers'), to reinforce the two knights, twenty serjeants, ten crossbowmen and twenty longbowmen of the castle garrison. This force, numbering about eighty, successfully dealt with their enemy on 14 September 1267, but not, apparently, without losing both men and horses. Roger may have been directly, or indirectly, involved with them, but seems to have avoided detection. There is nothing to suggest that the threat to seize all his lands in such circumstances was carried out.[12]

Roger may have kept his head down in the late 1260s, but he is unlikely to have been contented. His lord, Robert de Ferrers, had been permanently deprived of his estates by Edmund, the King's son, in 1269, and he must have found the redemption of his own lands a tiresome burden. By 1270 he was leading a band of outlaws whose depredations ranged across several counties into Wiltshire, and whose activities were described in some detail when the law finally caught up with him five years later. He was accused of being responsible for many burglaries, murders, arsons and robberies committed in Leicestershire, Nottinghamshire and Wiltshire, his worst crime being an attack on Stanley Abbey (Wiltshire) on 29 September 1270 during which he had stolen a large sum of money together with horses and other valuables and killed one of the monks. Roger denied all the charges except those committed before 10 December 1266 which were covered by the pardon granted him on that date. He had, he said, been loyal to the King since then, and asked that his case be tried by juries from the three counties named.[13]

Any one of these allegations would have merited the death penalty, and Roger would have been obliged to deny them to have had any hope of avoiding conviction. Stanley is a long way from Swannington, and he may have thought that he would not be recognized there or, if the worst came to the worst, he could always plead mistaken identity. Untruthfulness, or pulling the wool over the eyes of his opponents, would have been part of his stock in trade, of course, but documents referring to the sixteen months he remained at liberty after the attack on the abbey make it clear that if this particular charge faltered, there were plenty of alternatives. Complaints that he was responsible for a series of assaults on vulnerable travellers, particularly churchmen, in Nottinghamshire, Leicestershire and Derbyshire, continued to reach London, and the King asked Reginald Grey to deal with the problem. Grey received a total of 200 marks, half lent by the Archbishop of York, Walter Giffard, and half by some Florentine merchants,[14] and 'later reported that he had pursued him [Godberd] from Nottingham to Derby to Hereford'[15] where he was captured some time before 11 February 1272. Leicester and Nottingham

49. This picture, ostensibly of Robin, was printed on the front of the *Gest of Robyn Hode and his meyne, and the proud Sheryfe of Nottingham* published in 1508, but had been used to depict Chaucer's yeoman seventeen years before.

50. Archery practice at the butts, from the Lutterell Psalter, *c*.1340. Could the hooded figure who has just scored a bullseye be Robin himself?

51. The gatehouse of Kirklees priory, where Robin is said to have been murdered, as it appeared in the nineteenth century.

52. 'Robin Hood and his
betrayer' (Berwick in Ritson).
Robin allowed the prioress to
bleed him for medicinal reasons,
but she deliberately bled him to
death.

53. Robin Hood's grave-slab at Kirklees, drawn by Nathaniel Johnson in 1665. From J.W. Walker,
The True History of Robin Hood (Wakefield, 1952).

54. Robin's grave at Kirklees as it would have appeared in the nineteenth century.

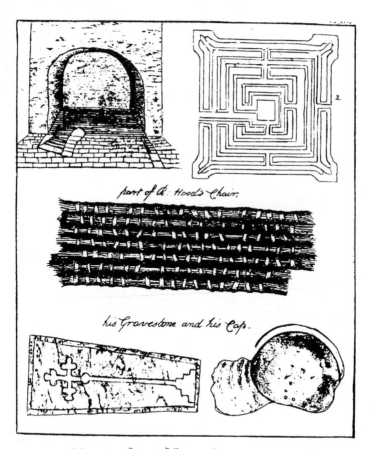

part of R. Hood's Chair.

his Gravestone and his Cap.

Robm Hood obüt xxiv kal Decembris mccxxxxvii

55. Robin Hood relics displayed at St Anne's Well, Nottingham, drawn by John Throsby (from R. Thoroton, *Antiquities of Nottingham* (1797). They include his cap, gravestone (compare with illustrations 20 and 53), and part of his chair.

56. Little John's original gravestone (actually a grave-slab) at Hathersage, a drawing showing details now almost worn away (compare with illustration 7).

57. Little John's Cottage at Hathersage, 1832. From J.W. Walker, *The True History of Robin Hood* (Wakefield, 1952).

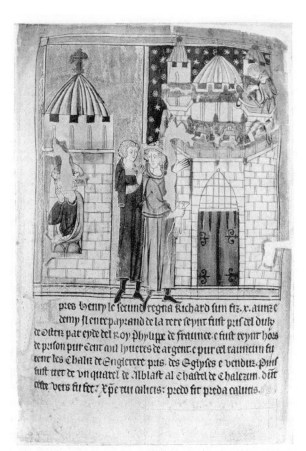

58. Richard I, the king most often associated with Robin Hood.

59. King John. Robin's loyalty to King Richard and opposition to John's attempt to usurp his brother's authority is a theme of many modern tales.

60. & 61. Edward I, who as Prince Edward was primarily responsible for Simon de Montfort's defeat and death at Evesham.

Left: 62. Simon de Montfort's seal.

Below: 63. Simon de Montfort's last fight at the battle of Evesham 4 August 1265.

64. The dismemberment of Earl Simon's body after the battle of Evesham, from B.L. Cotton MS. Nero D ii, f. 177.

65. Kenilworth Castle keep, as it would have looked when de Montfort's supporters were besieged there in 1266.

66. Nottingham Castle, a reconstruction based on archaeological evidence and analogous architecture elsewhere.

67. An eleventh-century archer. Archery appealed to all social classes, and Englishmen hunted and sported with the bow long before they used it to win great victories in the Hundred Years' War.

68. An eleventh-century Old English calendar showing agricultural scenes typical of the months between May and August. Roger Godberd, who was a gentleman-farmer when he was not causing trouble, would have been familiar with the work-patterns shown here.

69. Louis Rhead's map of the royal forests, from his *Bold Robin Hood and His Outlaw Band. Their Famous Exploits in Sherwood Forest* (1912). Barnsdale was south of York and the river Ouse, much smaller, and closer to Sherwood, than shown here.

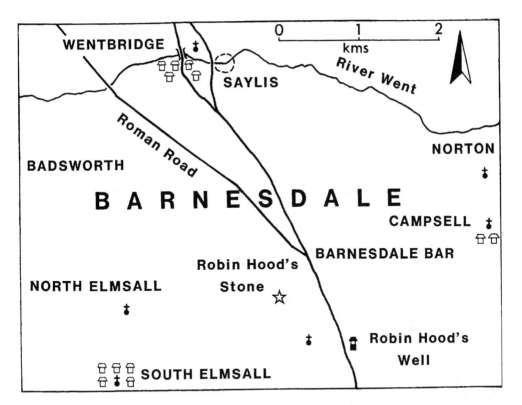

Above: 70. Map of Barnesdale forest showing Robin's well, stone, and places mentioned in the ballads.

Right: 71. This drawing by Howard Pyle is based on a 'prequel' describing Robin's first encounter with his future lieutenant Little John, one that proved to be both painful and embarrassing! The Robin of the ballads was a brilliant archer, but could sometimes be worsted in other ways.

Above: 72. Sir Richard at the Lee has refused to surrender Robin and his men to the sheriff, and so the latter rides to London to explain the situation to the king in person. Another scene from the *Geste*.

Left: 73. Little John has taken service with the sheriff, and quarrels with the cook when the latter refuses to serve him his dinner. They fight for an hour, earning one another's respect in the process, and the cook finally agrees to join John in the woods.

Right: 74. Robin meets Will Scarlett for the first time. Howard Pyle portrays him as a rather foppish individual, but there is no evidence for this in the earliest ballads.

Below: 75. The knight pretends to plead for more time to pay, knowing that the abbot and the justice he has bribed to assist him will refuse. They do not know that he has Robin's money in his pocket, and will not forfeit his lands after all.

Merry·Robin·stops·a·Sorrowful·Knight:

76. Robin encounters the knight whose son has committed murder and who cannot afford to repay the money he has borrowed to save him. The story makes it clear that the outlaws are not opposed to entire classes in society – only to individuals within them who misuse their power.

were required to repay the archbishop thirty-five marks each while Derbyshire contributed the remaining thirty, and the merchants were similarly reimbursed in equal shares.

It seems likely that Godberd's gang had increased in size, drawing in other brigands and malcontents, as he became more notorious, and one of his partners in crime was a certain Walter Devyas (or Denyas or de Ewyas). Devyas is first noticed in February 1269 when he was pardoned the murder of one William fuiz le Chapeleyn (William, son of the chaplain), 'as it appears... that he is not guilty',[16] but this let-off did not make him any more law-abiding. He apparently joined Godberd in his depredations in various places, and in October 1271 the Yorkshire knight Sir Richard Foliot was ordered 'to conduct Walter Deuyas [yet another variation!] charged with divers trespasses to the king'.[17] This sounds like a straightforward enough matter, but Foliot declined to obey the instruction and was shortly afterwards accused of harbouring Devyas, Godberd 'and other wrongdoers' in his castle at Fenwick (Yorkshire). The sheriff of Yorkshire was ordered to seize his lands as a way of compelling him to submit to justice, and Foliot was obliged to surrender both the castle and his son Edmund as sureties that he would present himself at York on an agreed day. Godberd, Devyas and the others had presumably slipped away before the sheriff arrived, and Foliot was either sent or decided to travel to Westminster where he threw himself on the royal mercy. He presented the King and Council with the names of twelve 'mainpernors' who would guarantee that he would appear in the Court of King's Bench to answer the charges on 13 October, whereupon Henry instructed the sheriff to return his lands to him. Most of his sureties were Yorkshiremen, some of them members of the old baronial party, but curiously, there were also two from Essex.[18]

Devyas and Foliot seem to have been treated rather leniently, and this may not be unconnected with their apparently cordial relationship with Prince Edward. Walter was pardoned the murder of William fuiz le Chapeleyn 'at the instance of Edward the king's son', and Henry allowed that Richard's case could be dealt with sooner 'if Edward, our first born son, returns more swiftly to England and wishes this business to be hastened'.[19] There is, unfortunately, no surviving plea roll for the Court of King's Bench for Michaelmas term 1272, and we cannot tell if, or when, Richard was held to account, but the death of the old King in November may have given him a breathing space. He was certainly in Edward's company – and clearly in favour – when Edward invaded Wales in 1277, and as late as October 1290 was appointed keeper of Horston Castle, to the north of Derby.[20] Godberd had been captured before his case came to court, and the authorities may have been concerned more to ensure good behaviour in future than to exact retribution for the mistakes of the past.

Devyas's subsequent career is uncertain because the surviving documents do not say precisely when the events they describe happened, but he continued his life of brigandage and was involved in an altercation – a small battle perhaps – at Thorpe Peverel (Perlethorpe, near Edwinstowe in Nottinghamshire) with Sir Roger Lestrange and others sent to catch him. No fewer than seventeen of Lestrange's men lost horses worth between ten marks (£6 13s 4d) and £20 each together with armour and equipment valued at £34 6s,[21] but in spite of this Walter was captured and brought to justice. The continuator of William of Newburgh's chronicle records that he was sentenced to death (the Prince clearly did not intercede for him on this occasion), and executed ('decollatus') at some point between the feast of St Peter ad Vincula on 1 August and the death of Henry III on 16 November 1272. Newburgh Priory is about twenty miles north of York, near Ampleforth, and it says much for Devyas's reputation that a monk confined to an abbey far from the scene of his activities had heard of him and thought his end worthy of note.[22]

According to these documents then, Godberd and Devyas were captured in separate incidents by different people in different places, the former by Reginald Grey before February 1272 and the other by Lestrange later in the year. There should therefore be nothing more to say of the matter, but a note in the Hundred Rolls for 3 Edward I (1275) states that they were both taken by Hugo de Babington at the North Grange of Rufford Abbey, near Blidworth in Nottinghamshire, and imprisoned in Nottingham Castle.[23] Some entries in the Hundred Rolls refer to events that occurred many years earlier, but it is difficult to avoid the conclusion that both men were apprehended twice in the 1270s in entirely different circumstances. It is impossible to say if they were captured by Babington first and by Grey and Lestrange second (or vice-versa), but the former seems more probable. Babington was under-sheriff of Nottingham in 1271, and it seems likely that he released them, or that they escaped, from his custody only to be re-taken a few months after returning to their old ways. It is curious that after Godberd was taken by Grey and imprisoned at Bruges in May 1272 he was not delivered from Hereford gaol (to which he had presumably been transferred in the interval), until December 1275,[24] but there is no evidence that he was at large or that he was arrested by Babington during this period. Walter Devyas certainly appears to have died in 1272 – there is nothing to suggest that he was alive later – and it is surely more probable that the two of them escaped or were released together, and were recaptured separately later, than the other way round. But whatever the circumstances, their careers as outlaws were effectively over by the end of this year.

Roger Godberd was finally sent to Newgate to stand trial in April 1276, and pleaded, as we noted above, that all his crimes had been committed in time of war and subsequently pardoned. The authorities are unlikely to have been swayed by this argument, but he was not executed (unlike the unfortunate Devyas), and was allowed to return home to Swannington after serving a further term of imprisonment. One of the consequences of this was that his family would have found themselves exposed and at the mercy of any who sought to take advantage of their predicament, and a patent of 6 Edward I (1278–9) records that one Radulph de Hengham was appointed to take the assize of novel disseisin arraigned by Roger, son of Roger Godberd, against Margaret de Ferrers, dowager Countess of Derby (Robert de Ferrers's mother), and others, touching a tenement in Shepshed in Charnwood ('Seepisheued in Charnewod').[25] Margaret was clearly taking advantage of the difficulties of both the Godberds and her own son to enforce a demand she would perhaps not have dared make in other circumstances, and young Roger's aim was to recover the property in the interim pending a full, legal investigation into her claim.

Margaret's death shortly before 12 March 1281 can only have assisted the Godberds' position, but there is other evidence that they remained well able to take care of themselves. In November 1275 (while Roger was in prison at Hereford), Lucy Grey complained that Thomas, son of Alan Huchun, Hugh in Thewro and some of her other servants had been attacked while attending to her affairs in Leicester:

Robert de Okham, Robert de Shepesheved, Geoffrey Godberd and others, issuing from the abbey of Leicester, killed Thomas and maimed Hugh and beat the others, and afterwards returned to the abbey and were received there.[26]

The abbot was accused of procuring the malefactors (literally, taking care of them), and they were all ordered to answer for their crimes.

Geoffrey Godberd was Roger's brother, Robert 'of Shepshed' a probable gang-member, while Lucy Grey was the widow of Reginald's kinsman, John Grey of Codnor (Derbyshire).[27] It was, of course, Reginald Grey who had been paid to apprehend Roger Godberd, his former comrade in the Nottingham Castle garrison, and this raises the possibility that the assault in Leicester was a revenge attack against a member of the extended Grey family. The gang would have found it harder to target Reginald or another senior figure directly, but hurting a man by damaging his assets was a concept as old as the Middle Ages themselves. In the last resort the dispute need be no more than one group of men settling a personal score with others who just happened to be Grey servants; but why was the Abbot of Leicester harbouring them? One is reminded of how the abbey's chronicler, Henry Knighton, did not exactly disapprove of the Folvilles' activities in the next century, and the abbot may well have had his own, local differences with the Greys.[28]

There is no indication of how long Roger Godberd remained a prisoner,[29] but he had been released – and was still very much alive and kicking – when the itinerant justices William de Vescy, Thomas de Normanville and Richard de Creppinges, heard cases relating to offences allegedly committed in Sherwood when they sat in

Nottingham in 1287. Roger, his brother Geoffrey, Reginald Grey, and a number of others were accused of poaching deer in Bulwell and Beskwood on various occasions when they were employed at Nottingham Castle in 1264. The justices had not visited the area since before this date, and obtaining reliable information and securing convictions after an interval of twenty-three years was bound to be difficult. Grey did not always appear when summoned, and then claimed he knew nothing about it. Roger and Geoffrey surrendered to the sheriff and may again have been briefly imprisoned since we are told that afterwards, Henry le Lou (another of the accused), 'came to the King's court and liberated this company from gaol'.[30] Le Lou apparently bailed them – there is no suggestion that he forced the prison – and they probably suffered little more than inconvenience.[31] Roger was apparently a law-abiding citizen by 1287, although he was by then approaching sixty years of age.

Medieval criminals seem to have had little difficulty in rejoining society when their days of flouting the law were behind them, and it is unlikely that Roger, Eustace de Folville or James Coterel died anywhere but in their beds.[32] Only a few of their associates seem to have paid the ultimate penalty, Eustace's brother Richard and Godberd's accomplice Walter Devyas among them, and perhaps they were unlucky rather than typical. We do not know if Roger had recovered all or most of the lands he had forfeited in the 1260s by the time of his death, or if his family could afford to provide him with a memorial. Swannington Church was rebuilt in the eighteenth century, and there are now no reminders of the Godberds either there or in the surrounding village. Scarcely anyone has heard of Roger Godberd and Walter Devyas, but are they still known to almost everyone – not as Godberd and Devyas but as Robin Hood and Little John?

II

THE REAL ROBIN HOOD

Roger Godberd was a Leicestershire yeoman farmer and Walter Devyas apparently no greater; but the sheer number of references to them in contemporary documents indicates that in their heyday they were known – feared and admired in equal measure – from Yorkshire in the north to Wiltshire in the south. They were not alone, of course. We have already seen something of other outlaws who enjoyed a like reputation in the Middle Ages, and the purpose of this chapter is to explain why Roger and Walter are more likely to have inspired the stories of Robin Hood and Little John than some better-known candidates. We cannot expect to find incontrovertible proof of this – no minstrel would admit to basing his tales on the activities of anyone other than his hero or heroes – but the greater the number of similarities or coincidences, the more certain the identification. Let us examine each one in turn.

There are many different Robin Hood ballads, but the setting, the 'floruit' as it is sometimes termed, is always consistent. Robin is an outlaw, a fine archer whose gang poaches the king's deer in Sherwood forest, who is at loggerheads with the sheriff, and who preys on wealthy travellers. Churchmen are not spared – on the contrary, they are a particular target – and rough justice is acceptable because it is the only justice which is fair. Roger Godberd found himself on the wrong side of the law on several occasions, the first as early as 1250 when he claimed that his mother and stepfather had wasted his woods at Swannington. He was in more trouble with Jordan le Fleming in the early 1260s, in the period after Lewes when he was granted protection and safe conduct, and again after the battle of Chesterfield and his attack on Garendon Abbey when he was assured that nothing would happen to him if he came to the King to 'treat of peace'. The terms of his pardon may have given him pause for reflection – at least, we hear nothing more of him for the next few years – but he was again a fugitive after attacking Stanley Abbey and committing other offences in 1270 and 1271. He was captured by Hugo de Babington, but escaped and was again at large until Reginald Grey ran him to earth in Hereford. It is worth noting that Babington imprisoned him in Nottingham Castle where Robin was incarcerated in *Robin Hood and the Monk*.

There is no evidence that Godberd was a particularly skilful archer – that part, at least, may be poetic licence – but he and his friends used bows and arrows when they poached game in Sherwood in 1264. It was alleged that on one day near Easter they killed hares, twenty-six stags, forty-five does and no fewer than one hundred and ten roe deer.[1] They may not have been able to 'slet the wande' as the ballad has it, but they were certainly not amateurs![2] Roger's depredations seem to have been committed principally in Sherwood rather than in his more local forest of Charnwood, and his pursuers Grey and Babington were both present or former sheriffs of Nottinghamshire and Derbyshire. Something had to be done to curb the 'outlaws, thieves and malefactors' who were responsible for 'so many and great homicides and robberies', and the authorities were in no doubt that he was their 'leader and captain', or alternatively, 'leader and master'.[3]

So far so good, then, but there must have been many brigands who used the forest as a cloak for their activities and who satisfy at least some of the Robin Hood criteria. The factors mentioned above would not really prove anything if they were all the evidence we had to go on, but fortunately there are several quite striking parallels between what is known of Roger Godberd's deeds and the earliest ballads. The Robin of the stories is devoted to Our Lady, but is frequently at loggerheads with wealthy and corrupt religious who have fallen far from the ideals of their founders. It is no coincidence that, at various times, he helps the knight outwit the Abbot of St Mary's, York, is betrayed by a monk (who is then killed by his followers), and is finally done to death by the Prioress of Kirklees. The attitude of those who composed the ballads towards people of this class in society could hardly be plainer, and Godberd's activities would have provided them with plenty of inspiration. The document describing his pursuit and capture by Reginald Grey affirms that while he was abroad 'no religious or other person could pass without being taken... and spoiled of his goods'[4] and we have already noticed his attacks on Garendon and Stanley abbeys. The Garendon episode is interesting because there is an obvious parallel between Roger's seizure of documents which proved that he had given the monastery rights over some of his properties, and Sir Richard at the Lee's less violent redemption of his lands from the Abbot of St Mary's, York.

The two Sir Richards – Sir Richard at the Lee of the ballads and the Yorkshire knight Sir Richard Foliot – are central to our story because one sheltered Roger Godberd's gang in his castle in exactly the same way that the other protected Robin and his 'merry men'. We saw in chapter one how the friendly knight was nearly hanged and then threatened with the loss of his estates for saving Robin and the wounded Little John from the pursuing sheriff, and subsequently, how Richard Foliot was held to account for harbouring Godberd, Devyas and others in his castle at Fenwick (Yorkshire) in February 1272. Foliot was a man of some substance in northern England – he was given right of free warren in three manors he held in Yorkshire together with two in Lincolnshire and one in Nottinghamshire in January 1252[5] – and Professor Holt has pointed out that he possessed not only Grimston and Wellow on the eastern bounds of Sherwood, but also Stubbs and Norton which, together with Fenwick, lay in the valley of the Went a mere six miles below Wentbridge. 'From his castle at Fenwick, of a spring evening, he would see the sun go down over Barnsdale, no more than five miles away.'[6]

The *Geste* describes the poor knight's castle as being double ditched and standing walled by the road, 'a lytell within the wode', a description which fits one of Richard Foliot's properties quite neatly. It is not, unfortunately, Fenwick where the trouble is said to have occurred, but Wellow which lay just outside the boundary of the royal forest but which was still very much a forest village. Wellow Castle (or Jordan Castle as it is known today), had only a single ditch, or moat, and was situated a quarter of a mile from the then road; but if the writer of the ballad was referring to the village the features match. The remains of a defensive ditch that originally encircled the place and which, according to Tony Molyneux-Smith, was double 'in the area of the gateway and drawbridge'[7], are still visible on the eastern and southern sides, and Wellow was – and is – located on the main road less than two miles from Ollerton. It is only a clue, but the probability is that the ballad writer had some real evidence before him and was not just inventing details as he went along.

Sir Richard at the Lee was in financial difficulties because he was trying to help his son who had killed 'a knight of Lancaster', and it is interesting that Sir Richard Foliot also sought clemency for persons accused of murder on at least two occasions. In December 1263 he secured a pardon for William, son of Thomas de Grimeston of Norton (presumably one of his tenants), who was responsible for the death of a Richard de Stapleton, and four years later interceded on behalf of Jordan de Bramwich who had killed John, Adam de Bramwich's son.[8] This last case is particularly interesting because Foliot himself had a son called Jordan, and the story would only have to be adjusted a little for Jordan de Bramwich to become the knight's son in the ballad. None of this proves that the two Sir Richards were indisputably one and the same person of course, but the coincidences are surely more than mere chance.

Foliot's involvement is yet another example of a supposed upholder of the law colluding with the law-breakers, and begs the question why was he was prepared to take such risks for them? He may have sympathized with the plight of former Montfortians – he had supported the baronial cause in 1261–2 before returning to the royal side a year later – but the most likely explanation is that he was related by marriage to Walter Devyas. Godberd and Devyas seem to have operated both together and separately, and no one actually describes Devyas as Godberd's 'lieutenant'; but there is a striking similarity between Devyas's murder of a chaplain's son called William[9] and Little John's slaying of the 'gret-hedid munke' in the *Robin Hood and the Monk*. Devyas was, as we have seen, pardoned 'at the instance' of Prince Edward, and although there is no evidence that either Walter or Roger were taken into the king's service it is easy to see how such stories developed. Both Godberd and the Robin of the ballads were forgiven, lived within the law for a time, and then returned to their former way of life.

The story of the monk, his betrayal of Robin, Robin's capture, and the vengeance wrought by Little John and Much, can also be compared with Roger Godberd's attack on Stanley Abbey, and with his brother Geoffrey's murderous assault on Lucy Grey's servants. We noted in chapter ten how the miscreants were being sheltered by the Abbot of Leicester, a man who, in the traditional scenario, would have been their enemy, but this is the only real difference between the two stories. Thomas Huchun was killed (like the monk), and his companions seriously injured, but there is no evidence that the perpetrators were brought to justice. Roger himself was held responsible for the death of the monk killed when his gang attacked Stanley, but still lived to enjoy a peaceful old age.

The first writer to connect Robin with the troubles of the 1260s was the Scottish abbot Walter Bower. Bower was writing almost 200 years later, but some of his remarks could apply equally to Roger Godberd. Robin, he says, was a 'famous murderer', a phrase that could just as readily describe Roger, and he and Little John plied their lawless trade 'together with their accomplices from among the dispossessed'.[10] In 1266:

> the dispossessed barons of England and the royalists were engaged in fierce hostilities. Among the former Roger Mortimer occupied the Welsh marches and John Daynil [d'Eyvill] the Isle of Ely; Robert Hood was now living in outlawry among the woodland copses and thickets. Between them they inflicted a vast amount of slaughter on the common and ordinary folk, cities and merchants.[11]

He goes on to say that King Henry and Prince Edward raised a large army and besieged Kenilworth where most of the nobles who were still resisting the King had taken refuge. The castle, with its towers and protecting walls, was virtually impregnable, and the defenders put up determined resistance. But eventually, they were worn down by starvation and surrendered on condition that they kept life and limb.

We do not know where Bower obtained his information, but the detail is remarkably accurate. Roger Mortimer was a marcher baron, John d'Eyvill resisted the King from Ely before marching on London with the Earl of Gloucester, and Kenilworth was defended and ultimately surrendered in exactly the way described. The abbot had no reason to 'invent' Robert Hood at this point in his narrative, and so we may assume that this piece of information came to him from the same reliable source as the rest. Roger Godberd may not have been among the defenders of Kenilworth, but Bower does not say that Robert Hood joined them either. There is no reason why the Robert described here and Roger should not be one and the same.

There is more. The Robin of the ballads is, as we have noted, a yeoman, a term which could refer to employees in noble and royal households as well as to under-foresters, but which was most usually applied to men on the highest rung of the non-aristocratic ladder. In the words of Professor Pollard 'not a gentleman, still a working farmer, artisan or tradesman who worked with his hands, he was nevertheless a man of local substance and importance, employing one or two of his own servants'.[12] The little we know of Roger Godberd's status in Swannington suggests that he too was a member of this class in society, someone who aspired to gentility and who was looking to add to his lands and financial resources by any means he could. It is also interesting that the fictional Robin made his peace with a King Edward. Henry III ruled England when Godberd was formally pardoned and admitted to the King's peace in 1266, but he did not finally shake off the consequences of his life of crime until he was released from prison in the late 1270s or early 1280s – well into the reign of Edward I. Another parallel is that both Roger and Robin ranged over wide areas and moved rapidly from place to place. There can be little doubt that they were both mounted, and Robin would not have been able to give the poor knight a fast courser and a palfrey (the latter to carry his equipment) if he had not had such animals readily available. They may have fought, or practised archery, on foot, but horses were essential for speed.

There are, of course, many aspects of the ballads that cannot be directly related to what is known of the exploits of Godberd and Devyas, and we must beware of making assumptions when there is no clear evidence one way or the other. Robin and Roger both targeted wealthy members of the religious establishment, but whereas Robin redeemed himself by his devotion to Our Lady, Roger does not seem to have had any such scruples. One reason may be simply that no one ever commented on Roger's personal piety (or lack of it), but it is distinctly possible that some of de Montfort's aura would have attached itself to those who fought for him or were associated with his cause after Evesham. The same is true of Robin's apparent lack of family and disinterest in women. Roger Godberd had a wife and children, but they are wholly absent from documents which describe his depredations. The vast probability is that Robin and his friends *did* have partners and relationships, but the ballad writers were not interested in them. They were neither heroines nor the cause of complaint.

Other possible differences are that Roger and Walter do not seem to have operated in Barnsdale; they did not, apparently, quarrel with one another (as Robin and Little John did in both *Robin Hood and the Monk* and *Robin Hood and Guy of Gisborne*); and there is nothing to suggest that John was executed or that Roger died from excessive bleeding. Any, or even all, of these things *could* be true however. Roger's life can only be glimpsed in what are almost exclusively official government and legal records. He left no will, wrote no letters (perhaps he was not even literate), and no one troubled to record what he was like or anything he said. It would be presumptuous to assume that because something is not mentioned it did not occur.

But if Roger Godberd was Robin Hood, why is he not called Robin Hood in at least one or more documents? The earliest use of the name in this context dates from 1261, the period of the baronial rebellion, but the handful of such cases that have come to light represent only a tiny fraction of the vast number of criminals dealt with in the period. It seems improbable that Roger was ever known as Robin in his lifetime, but this is hardly surprising in the circumstances. What is more significant is the subsequent growth of the legend as represented by the ballads. There can be no doubt that stories or 'rhymes' of Robin Hood were popularized during the early fourteenth century, and were widely known when Langland wrote *The Vision of Piers Plowman* in the 1360s or 1370s. The writers drew on many sources and doubtless sought inspiration where they could find it. Tales of Fulk Fitzwarin, Eustace the Monk and others were plundered for stories that provided good entertainment, and recent events that had fired the popular imagination, the rebellions of Simon de Montfort and Thomas of Lancaster for example, also yielded rich pickings.

In one sense then, the Robin of the ballads could be Fulk, Eustace, Hereward or any of the other popular outlaws, or even Eustace de Folville or James Coterel. They were all admired by sections of the population, and were, to a greater or lesser extent, the stuff of legend. Simon de Montfort was commemorated in song and regarded as a popular saint for perhaps fifty years after his death, and a similar cult of Thomas of Lancaster developed after his execution in 1322. The circumstances of Lancaster's death may have allowed a younger generation to transfer their admiration to someone they could actually remember, and it was always likely that those who had refused to submit to tyranny would be singled out for particular admiration. Roger Godberd may, in reality, have been fighting as much for himself and for Robert de Ferrers, his immediate overlord, as for the baronial 'cause', and was almost forgotten as de Montfort's own posthumous popularity faded: but he and his associates had made enough of an impression for some their deeds to pass into legend and become an integral part of the ballads. The character of Robin Hood has drawn on many sources over the centuries (and continues to do so), but there are enough similarities to conclude that Roger's career lies at the heart of it. He, for one, would be surprised by that.

APPENDIX 1:
GAMELYN & ADAM BELL

Gamelyn, together with Adam Bell and his friends Clyn of the Clough and William of Cloudisley, may have rivalled Robin Hood's popularity in the late Middle Ages, although few people have heard of them today. They were almost certainly legendary, but their fictional careers may have contributed to, or borrowed from, stories told of Robin and they deserve a brief mention here.

The *Tale of Gamelyn* was probably composed about the middle of the fourteenth century, and so stands between the stories that grew up around outlaws like Fulk and Hereward, and the earliest recorded ballads of Robin. It is, however, closer to the latter in that the magic and fantasy of the earlier legends has given way to an altogether starker reality. Gamelyn's forest is, like Robin's, a place where 'the wandering fugitive feels the pinch of hunger' and 'where one stumbles and tears one's clothes'.[1] Fulk, Hereward and the others were aristocrats who would never have joined in archery contests like Robin, or, like Gamelyn, fought a wrestling champion at a local fair.

The story opens at the death-bed of an old knight, Sir Johan of Boundys, who divides his estate between his three sons. Gamelyn, the youngest, is not old enough to inherit his share immediately, and subsequently finds that his eldest brother has not only wasted the property but refuses to give him any part of it. The quarrel that ensues is characterized by an almost unbelievable naivety on the one hand and by extreme violence on the other. On one occasion, when Gamelyn has his brother at his mercy, he allows himself to be bound hand and foot because this is what his brother had sworn to do to him and he does not want his brother to be dishonoured. Something like this could only happen in a poem, but there is nothing touching or unreal about the way in which Gamelyn deals with those who cross him. The wrestling champion has his arm and ribs smashed, a porter who tries to prevent the young Turk from entering his brother's house has his neck broken, abbots and priors (his brother's guests, who have refused to plead for him), are badly beaten,[2] and those who presume to judge him – his brother, a justice and twelve jurors – are 'hanged hye'.

Gamelyn is evidently a more trusting, as well as a more violent, man than Robin, but their stories still touch at a number of points. Both lead bands of outlaws in the forest, although it is only a temporary refuge for Gamelyn the prospective landowner. Both are prepared to abuse senior churchmen, and both are concerned for those who suffer at the hands of the system. Gamelyn is anxious for his tenants who are at his brother's mercy, and, like Sir Richard at the Lee, he is a member of the knightly class threatened by the loss of his lands. Both he and Robin kill the sheriff (Gamelyn's brother had been pricked as sheriff), and both are subsequently taken into royal service, although Gamelyn's appointment as chief justice of the forest could again, only happen in a story. There are even two wrestling matches, with the same prizes of a ram and a ring. Right always triumphs, and the villains get their just deserts.

Adam Bell has been dated to the beginning of the sixteenth

century, but is almost certainly much older. It has a different location
to the Robin Hood ballads, Inglewood forest in Cumberland, but
incorporates much of the familiar, traditional material. One of
the three outlaws, William of Cloudisley, decides, against Adam's
advice, to visit his wife in Carlisle, but is betrayed and captured. He
is sentenced to be executed, but is rescued by Adam and Clyn who
gain access to Carlisle by murdering the gatekeeper and then shoot
the sheriff and the justice in the market-place. This is too close to
Robin Hood and the Monk (in which Little John and Much free
Robin by killing the porter), and to the rescue of Sir Richard at the
Lee in the *Geste*, to be mere coincidence; and so is their decision
to immediately throw themselves on the king's mercy. The queen
persuades her husband to forgive them (queens could, and often
did, intercede for subjects in difficulty in the Middle Ages), and they
have their pardons before word of their crimes reaches the court.
Such trickery would not merit reward in most circumstances; but
after William has split an apple set upon his son's head from sixty
paces the queen gives him cloth and fee, his wife is summoned to
become her chief gentlewoman and governess of the royal nursery,
and his two friends are appointed yeomen of her chamber. It is the
old theme of the outlaws' fundamental loyalty being recognized
and appreciated by the highest in the land.

The similarities between these stories and Robin's are obvious,
but there are also differences. *Gamelyn* and *Adam Bell* have
none of the 'disguisings' or waylaying of wealthy travellers that
the ballads have borrowed from tales of Fulk Fitzwarin and
earlier outlaws. There are no potters lending their pots, no bad
monks, and no fights with cooks. Gamelyn's relationship with his
brothers, and William of Cloudisley's wife and child, are central
to their stories, but Robin's family and romantic attachments are

passed over in silence. William splits a hazel wand at 400 paces just as Robin might have done, but Professor Holt points out that shooting at an apple perched on his son's head (like William Tell), has its origins in Icelandic saga. This, he suggests, is unsurprising given that Carlisle has access to the Irish Sea and the Isles, but it 'reinforces the impression that the story is more peripheral... not only geographically but also in its literary sources, social context and potential audience'.[3] A good story was always worth retelling – an audience would probably have been disappointed if some favourite and anticipated themes had not been included – but they have little to do with the real, historical Robin Hood.

APPENDIX 2: SELECTED DOCUMENTS

1. 1250. Roger Godberd complains, unavailingly, that his mother and step-father have wasted his lands. G.F. Farnham, *Leicestershire Medieval Village Notes*, 6 vols. (Leicester 1928–33), iv, p. 190.

Curia Regis Roll 141. Trinity, 34 Henry III, 1250, m. 13, Leyc. Anketil de Swaninton and Margaret, his wife, were attached to answer Roger Godebert in a plea of having made waste, sale and destruction of woods which they hold as dower of Margaret, of the inheritance of the said Roger in Swaninton. Roger complains that they made waste of 60 oaks, damage 100s. Anketil and Margaret come and deny waste and put themselves on the country. Roger does likewise. The inquisition say that they made no waste; therefore Anketil and Margaret are quit. Roger is not amerced because he is under age.

2. 1260. Roger Godberd demises his manor to Jordan le Fleming then ejects him by force. G.F. Farnham, *Leicestershire Medieval Village Notes*, 6 vols. (Leicester 1928–33), iv, p. 190.

Curia Regis Roll 168. Mich., 44/45 Henry III, 1260, m. 16 d. Leyc. Jordan le Fleming v. Roger Godeberd in a plea wherefore, since the said Roger demised to Jordan his manor of Swaninton for a term of 10 years, and the same Jordan had not held the manor for one whole year, the said Roger ejected Jordan from the said manor with force and arms, and took and carried away Jordan's goods and chattels to the value of £20. Roger did not appear. Order for attachment.

3. 1287. Roger Godberd and others are accused of poaching venison in Sherwood Forest in 1264 (extract from *The Sherwood Forest Book*, ed. H.E. Boulton, Thoroton Society xxiii (1964), p. 129. Translated by Tina Hampson).

Item Warinus de Bassingburne, qui obiit, Riginaldus de Grei et eorum homines ceperunt unum cervum cum leporariis suis in campo de Bullewell' et unum alium cervum in Beskwode die Lune proxima ante festum sancti Laurencii anno eodem, et tulerunt venacionem usque Bassingburne. Item predictus Riginaldus et homines sui ceperunt unum cervum et unum damum in bosco de Bullewell die Sabbatica proxima post festum sancti Bartholomei anno predicto et tulerunt venacionem ad castrum predictum, et ii damas in bosco de Novo loco in vigilo sancti Egidii anno predicto et tulerunt venacionem ad castrum predictum. Requisiti qui fuerunt in societate predictorum, Riginaldi et Waryni dicunt quod Willelmus le Wasteneys, qui obiit, Sthephanus frater eius, Robertus le Lou miles, Radulphus le Boteller miles, Willelmus de Mungumry pater, Willelmus de Maysam, Ricardus de Gaham parsona of Schirlond, Wyotus de Sandiacre, Rogerus Gootbert, Galfridus fratus eius, [and fourteen others]. Qui predicti Ricardus et (Sthephanus) (alii) non venerunt nec prius etc., set testatum est quod idem Sthephanus manet in comitatu Lyncolnie; idio presentatum est vicecomiti etc. ut supra. Et Robertus le Lou habet terras in comitatu Northt' idio presentatum est vicecomiti etc. Et Rogerus Gootberd et Galfridus frater eius habent terras in comitatu Leycestr'; idio presentatum est vicecomiti etc., [and so on].

(Translation). Item, Warin de Bassingburne who had died, Reginald de Grei and their men took one stag with their greyhounds in the field of Bullewell and one other stag in Beskwode on Monday next before the feast of St Lawrence in the same year, and took the venison as far as Bassingburne. Item, the aforesaid Reginald and his men took one stag and one deer in the wood of Bullewell on Saturday next after the feast of St Bartholomew in the aforesaid year and brought the venison to the aforesaid castle [Nottingham], and two deer in the wood of Novo Loco on the eve of St Giles in the aforesaid year and brought the venison to the aforesaid castle. Having been asked who were in the company of the aforesaid Reginald and Warin, they say that William le Wasteneys, who has died, Stephen his brother, Robert le Lou, knight, Ralph le Boteller, knight, William de Mungumry, father, William de Maysam, Richard de Gaham, parson of Schirlond, Wyotus de Sandiacre, Roger Gootbert, Geoffrey his brother [and fourteen others]. Which aforesaid Richard and Stephen and the others have not come and not previously, etc, but it is witnessed that the same Stephen remains in the county of Lincoln. Therefore it is presented to the sheriff, etc, as above. And Robert le Lou has lands in the county of Northamptonshire. Therefore it is presented to the sheriff etc. And Roger Gootberd and Geoffrey his brother have lands in the county of Leicestershire. Therefore it is presented to the sheriff, etc.

4. Roger Godberd's reputation, and capture by Reginald Grey. 11 February 1272. *Calendar of the Patent Rolls, Henry III, 1266–1272* (1913), p. 622.

Whereas on the showing of the magnates of the council and the complaint of many others the king lately understood that in the counties of Nottingham, Leicester and Derby, as well in the common ways as in the woods, numbers of robbers, on horseback and on foot, were abroad and that no religious or other person could pass without being taken by them and spoiled of his goods, and perceiving that without greater force and stouter pursuit these could not be taken or driven from the counties, he, after consultation with the council, ordered that 100 marks should be levied of the said counties and paid to Reynold de Grey to attach them; and whereas the said Reynold has pursued them manfully and captured one Roger Godberd, their leader and master, and delivered him to prison, and W. archbishop of York, has delivered 100 marks of his own to the said Reynold as the king ordered, the king wills that the sum shall be levied of the said counties, to wit, 35 marks of Nottingham, 35 marks of Leicester and 30 marks of Derby, and paid to the archbishop for his loan so made, and commands all persons of the counties to contribute their proportions and to be intending to their sheriffs, who have been commanded to levy the same and deliver it to the archbishop, in levying this.

5. Richard Foliot is accused of harbouring Roger Godberd, Walter Devyas, and others. *Calendar of the Close Rolls, Henry III 1268–1272* (1938), p. 462.

Manucaptores domini Ricardi Folyot quod veniet coram domino rege in quindena Sancti Michaelis anno regni regis lvij°. facturus et recepturus justiciam super hiis que sibi imponuntur tam super receptamento Walteri Devyas, Rogeri Godberd et aliorum malefactorum quam aliis secundum consideracionem curie domini regis; Scilicet, Johannes filius Johannis, Robertus de Estutevill', Baldewynus de Akeny, Walterus de Colevill', Philippus de Colevill', Johannes de Haveresham, Robertus de Affagaz de comitatu Essex', Ricardus de la Vache, Herbertus de Sancto Quintino, Gilbertus de Clovill', Rogerus de Leukenore, Walterus de Bures in comitatu Essex'.

'Ista cognicio facta fuit in presencia domini W. Eboracensis archiepiscopi, domini G. de Clar', comitis Gloucestr' et comitis Surreye, et aliorum de consilio regis.'

'Memorandum de negocio domini comitis Warenn'.

'Rex vicecomiti Ebor' salutem. Cum Ricardus Folyot de receptamento Walteri de Euyas, Rogeri Godberd et aliorum malafactorum rettatus fuisset, occasione cujus retti terras et tenementa ipsius Ricardi in balliva tua cepisti in manum nostrum et insuper as castrum suum de Fenwyk' accecisti ad capiendum eum, propter quod idem Ricardus castrum suum predictum et Edmundum filium ejus tradidit in ostagium, tali scilicet condicione, quod veniret coram te apud Eboracum ad certum diem inter te et ipsum super hoc prefixum, ad reddendum se prisone nostre, et idem Ricardus personaliter comparens coram nobis et consilio nostro apud Westmonasterium invenerit nobis manucaptores subscriptos, videlicet Johannem filium Johannis, Robertum de Stutevill', Baldewynum de Akeny, Walterum de Colevill', Philippum de Colevill', Johannem de Haveresham, Robertum de Affagaz de comitatu Essex', Ricardum de la Wache, Herbertum de Sancto Quintino, Gilbertum de Clovill', Rogerum de Leukenore et Walterum de Bures de comitatu Essex' veniendi coram nobis a die Sancti Michaelis in quindecim dies, vel, si Edwardus primogenitus noster citius in Anglia redierit et velit hoc negocium maturari, ad certum diem quem eidem Ricardo legitime duxerimus prefigendum, ad standum recto in curia nostra de predicto receptamento ei imposito, prout de jure debuerit secundum legem et consuetudinem regni nostri; tibi precipimus quod eidem Ricardo terras et tenementa sua predicta sic capta sine dilacione liberari facias in forma predicta. Teste rege apud Westmonasterium xvij. die Februarii.

(Translation). The mainpernors of lord Richard Folyot, that he should come before the lord king in the quindene of St Michael in the 57th year of the reign of the king, to make and receive justice concerning those things, which were imposed on him both concerning the harbouring of Walter Devyas, Roger Godberd and other wrongdoers and also concerning other things according to the consideration of the court of the king; namely John, son of John, Robert de Estutevill, Baldwin de Akeny, Walter de Colevill, Philip de Colevill, John de Haveresham, Robert de Affagaz of the county of Essex, Richard de la Vache, Herbert de St Quintin, Gilbert de Clovill, Roger de Leukenore, Walter de Bures in the county of Essex.'

'That acknowledgement was made in the presence of lord W., archbishop of York, lord G. de Clare, earl of Gloucester and earl of Surrey, and others of the king's council.'

'Memorandum about the business of the lord earl of Warenn.'

'The king, to the sheriff of York, greetings. Whereas Richard Folyot had been indicted of the harbouring of Walter de Euyas, Roger Godberd and other wrongdoers, by occasion of which indictment you took the lands and tenements of the same Richard in your bailiwick into our hands, and in addition you came to his castle of Fenwyk to capture him, on account of which the same Richard handed over his aforesaid castle and Edmund his son as a hostage, namely with such a condition that he should come before you at York at a certain day, fixed in advance between you and him concerning this, to surrender himself to our prison, and the same Richard, personally appearing before us and our council at Westminster, found for us the below-written mainpernors, namely, John, son of John, Robert de Stutevill, Baldwin de Akeny, Walter de Colevill, Philip de Colevill, John de Haveresham, Robert de Affagaz of the county of Essex, Richard de la Wache, Herbert de St Quintin, Gilbert de Clovill, Roger de Leukenore and Walter de Bures of the county of Essex, to come before us in the quindene after the day of St Michael, or, if Edward, our first-born son, returns more swiftly to England and wishes this business to be hastened, at a certain day, which we consider is to be lawfully fixed in advance for the same Richard, to stand trial in our court concerning the aforesaid harbouring imposed on him, just as he ought lawfully to do according to the law and custom of our kingdom; we order you that you cause his aforesaid lands and tenements thus taken to be delivered to the same Richard without delay in the aforesaid form. Witnessed by the king at Westminster on the 17th day of February.

6. Roger Godberd is accused of various crimes and tries to excuse himself. TNA JUST 1/1222, m. 15 (1275). Transcribed and translated by Lesley Boatwright.

Deliberacio Gaole Heref' facta per preceptum Domini Regis de Rogero Godberd coram W. de Helynn associato sibi Rogero de Burghill die sancti Stephani anno regni regis Edwardi quarto

Heref'. Idem Rogerus rettatus tanquam pupplicus latro de pluribus burgariis homicidiis incendiis et roberiis per ipsum factis in Comitatibus Leyc' Notingh' et Wiltes et precipue de hoc quod ipse una cum aliis malefactoribus nequiter depredatus fuit Abbatiam de Stanleye in predicto Comitatu Wiltes de quadam magna pecunie summa, equis et aliis rebus ibidem inventis et eciam de morte cuiusdam monachi ibi interfecti circiter festum sancti Michaelis anno regni domini regis Henrici patris domini regis nunc L° iiij° , venit et defendit omnes burgarios homicidia incendia roberias et omne latrocinium etc. preterquam tempore turbacionis nuper in Regno habite inter predictum dominum Henricum et Simonem quondam Comitem Leyc' et complices suos. Et unde dicit quod idem dominus Henricus rex recepit eum ad pacem suam eet perdonavit ei quicquid fecerat contra pacem suam etc. usque ad nonum diem Decembris anno regni sui L° primo. Ita quod extunc fideliter se haberet erga ipsum regem et heredes suos etc. et profert litteras patentes ipsius Henrici que hoc idem testantur. Et dicit quod ipse semper postea bene et fideliter se habuit erga predictum Regem heredes suos et quoscumque alios et quod non est culpabilis de aliquo premissorum et de hoc ponit se de bono et malo super patriam predictorum Comitatuum. Ideo preceptum est vicecomitibus predictorum Comitatuum quod venire faciant quilibet de Comitatu suo coram J. de Cobbeham (Justiciario ad Gaolam de Newegate deliberandam[i]) [marginated: Lond'] apud London a die Pasch' in tres septimanas xij etc. per quos etc. Et qui etc. ad recognoscendum in forma predicta. Quia etc. Et mandatum est vicecomiti Heref' quod venire faciat ibidem predictum Rogerum ad prefatum terminum.

(Translation). Delivery of the Gaol of Hereford, made by command of the Lord King, of Roger Godberd, before W. de Helynn (with Roger de Burghill associated with him) on St Stephen's Day,[1] in the fourth year of the reign of King E[dward I]

Hereford. The same Roger, accused as a public criminal[2] of many burglaries, homicides, arsons and robberies committed by him in the counties of Leics, Notts and Wilts, and especially accused that he, together with other evildoers, wickedly robbed the Abbey of Stanley in the said county of Wiltshire of a great sum of money, horses, and other things found there, and also of the death of a certain monk killed there about the feast of St Michael in the 54th year of the reign of the lord king Henry, father of the present lord king [29 Sept 1270], comes and denies all burglaries, homicides, arsons, robberies and all larceny etc., except at the time of the disturbance recently happening in the kingdom between the lord king Henry and Simon, former earl of Leicester, and his accomplices. And whereof he says that the same lord king Henry received him into his peace and pardoned him for whatever he had done against his peace etc. up till the ninth day of December in the 51st year of his reign [1266], on condition that from then on he would conduct himself faithfully towards the king and his heirs, etc., and he puts forward letters patent of the same king Henry which bear witness to this same. And he says that he has always thereafter conducted himself well and faithfully towards the said king and his heirs and everybody else, and that he is not guilty of any of the foregoing, and for good and ill he puts himself on the country of the aforesaid counties.[3] And so the sheriffs of the aforesaid counties were instructed to cause, each from his own county, 12 men to come before J. de Cobbeham, (justice appointed to deliver Newgate Gaol) at London [marginated: London] three weeks after Easter to decide the matter. [There now follow, in shortened form, the standard formulae – 12 jurors by whom the matter will be considered, who are not related to the parties, because the defendant has asked for a jury trial.] And the sheriff of Hereford was instructed to cause the said Roger to come there on the said date.

THE PRINCIPAL EVENTS OF THE
ROBIN HOOD ERA

1189 Henry II dies and Richard I (the Lionheart) succeeds to the throne.

1190–2 The Third Crusade.

1199 Death of Richard I and accession of King John.

1204 Normandy, ruled by the English kings since the Conquest, is recaptured by King Philip of France.

1208 John refuses to accept Stephen Langton as Archbishop of Canterbury and England is placed under papal interdict (until 1213).

1214 John's hopes of recovering Normandy are shattered at the battle of Bouvines.

1215 John concedes the Great Charter (Magna Carta), but then reneges on his undertaking.

1216 King Philip's son, Louis, arrives to take the English throne. John reacts vigorously, but dies at Newark in October. Henry III succeeds, aged nine.

1217 William Marshal defeats the French and ends the civil war.

1221 The first friars arrive in England.

1225 'Robertus Hode, fugitive' of Yorkshire is mentioned in official documents.

1236 Henry III marries Eleanor of Provence.

1238 Eleanor, the King's sister, marries Simon de Montfort.

1239 Birth of Prince Edward (Edward I).

1242 Henry III launches an expensive and unsuccessful war to regain England's lost possessions in France.

1254 King Henry accepts the Pope's offer of the throne of Sicily on behalf of his younger son, Edmund 'Crouchback', but attempts to install Edmund end in failure.

1258 The barons, alarmed by Henry's foreign adventures, compel him to accept the 'Provisions of Oxford' limiting his authority.

1259 Henry signs the Treaty of Paris ending the conflict with France, but throws off the restraints imposed by the Provisions by 1261.

1261 The first known instance of a criminal's name being changed to 'Robehod'.

1263 The barons agree to submit their differences with Henry to Louis IX's arbitration, but resort to arms when Louis's judgement, the 'Mise of Amiens', is given in Henry's favour.

1264 The barons defeat and capture Henry and Prince Edward at Lewes in May. Simon de Montfort becomes the effective ruler of England.

1265 De Montfort summons burgesses to attend Parliament for the first time (February), but is defeated and killed at Evesham in August.

1266 The 'Dictum of Kenilworth' restores Henry's full powers while allowing former rebels to be reconciled on terms.

1272 Henry III dies. Edward I succeeds to the throne.

1282 Rebellion in Wales. Edward conquers the principality and formally annexes it to England (1284).

1284 The future Edward II is born at Caernarvon Castle.

1290 Edward's wife, Eleanor of Castile, dies at Harby in Lincolnshire. The 'Eleanor Crosses' are erected at the places her body rests overnight on its way to Westminster.

1292 John Balliol becomes King of Scotland after Edward arbitrates in the succession.

1296 Balliol rebels and is deposed. Edward takes the government of Scotland into his own hands and transfers the Stone of Destiny from Scone to Westminster.

1297 William Wallace defeats the English at Stirling Bridge, but is worsted at Falkirk the following year.

1301 Edward of Caernarvon is created Prince of Wales.

1305 Wallace is captured and executed after a mock trial.

1306 Robert Bruce is crowned King of Scotland, but becomes a fugitive after his defeat at the battle of Methven.

1307 Bruce wins battle of Loudon Hill. Edward again marches northwards but dies near Carlisle on 7 July.

1308 Edward II marries Isabella of France. The Knights Templar are suppressed in England after being arrested in France the previous year.

1310 After an unsuccessful campaign in Scotland Parliament appoints Lords Ordainers, twenty-one bishops and peers, to reform the government and regulate the King's household.

1312 The future Edward III is born at Windsor Castle.

1314 Robert Bruce defeats Edward's larger army at the battle of Bannockburn and secures Scotland's independence.

1316 Joseph Hunter's 'Robert Hode' is mentioned in the Wakefield court rolls.

1318 After the Scots threaten northern England, the magnates force Edward to govern with a supervisory council (the Treaty of Leake).

1321 Edward favours Hugh Despenser and his son and namesake, provoking Earl Thomas of Lancaster and others to try to remove them by force.

1322 Thomas of Lancaster is defeated at Boroughbridge and executed afterwards.

1323 A Robyn Hode serves in the royal household.

1325 Queen Isabella fails to return from a visit to France, and mounts an invasion with the aid of her lover, Roger Mortimer.

1326 Edward is captured and the Despensers are executed.

1327 Edward is formally deposed and agrees to abdicate in his son's favour, but is subsequently murdered at Berkeley Castle.

1377 Langland refers to 'rymes of Robyn Hood' in *Piers Plowman*.

NOTES & REFERENCES

References are given in full on the first occasion in which they appear in each chapter but in shortened form thereafter.

Prologue: Robin Hood's World

1. K.B. McFarlane, 'Had Edward I a 'Policy' Towards the Earls', *The Nobility of Medieval England* (Oxford, 1973). Although McFarlane argued elsewhere that only an undermighty king had overmighty subjects.

2. When one man held one or more knight's fees there was no problem; but if there were say, twenty co-holders of a single fee which of them was liable for military service? Human nature being what it is they probably left it to one another, and the feudal host was never summoned after 1327.

3. Two excellent examples of this can be found in *English Historical Documents*, vol. 3 (1189–1327), ed. H. Rothwell (1965), nos. 197 ('A Wedding Brawl', 1268), and 198 (Christmas in Acton Scott, Shropshire, 1287). Note how in both cases the perpetrators were both drunk and armed – always a recipe for the worst!

1. Tales of Robin Hood

1. Some authorities consider that *Robin Hood and the Sheriff* and *Little John and the Sheriff* may have been a single ballad, *Robin Hood, Little John and the Sheriff.*

2. More precisely *monk,* because in the course of this part of the story the two monks inexplicably become one.

3. William Langland, *The Vision of Piers Plowman,* ed. A.V.C. Schmidt (Everyman, 1995), p. 82.

4. J.C. Holt, *Robin Hood* (1989), p. 142.

5. S. Knight, *Robin Hood, A Complete Study of the English Outlaw* (1994), pp. 264–5.

6. *The Paston Letters A.D. 1422–1509,* ed. J. Gairdner, 6 vols. (1904), v, p. 185.

7. Knight, *Robin Hood,* p. 272.

8. Holt, *Robin Hood,* p. 115.

9. *Ibid.,* p. 184.

10. Professor Pollard suggests that Robin's divine love for Our Lady was replaced by his romantic love for Marian after the Reformation. *Imagining Robin Hood* (2004), p. 189.

11. Richard Grafton, *Chronicle at Large* (1569), p. 84, quoted at greater length by S. Knight, *Robin Hood,* p. 40.

12. Originally, an outlaw could be slain with impunity; but by the thirteenth century he did not automatically lose his claim to his inheritance, and his killer could be charged with homicide. See M. Keen, *The Outlaws of Medieval Legend* (1961), p. 10.

13. Keen, *Outlaws,* p. 92 & p. 173.

2. Myth & Reality

1. M. Keen, *The Outlaws of Medieval Legend* (1961), p. 51. The comparisons are based on those noted by G. Phillips & M. Keatman, *Robin Hood. The Man Behind the Myth* (1995), pp. 116–21.

2. Keen, *Outlaws*, p. 54.

3. A.J. Pollard, *Imagining Robin Hood* (2004), p. 209.

4. Keen, *Outlaws*, p. 116, Pollard, *Robin Hood*, p. 82, S. Knight, *Robin Hood, A Complete Study of the English Outlaw* (1994), p. 81.

5. The change was a by-product of the Hundred Years' War that began in 1336. The slightly wealthier squires who could afford military equipment distanced themselves from their yeoman cousins, and esquire became a social distinction which, like knighthood, could be conferred by the king.

6. Although this has not prevented at least one serious historian from treating parts of some later ballads as factual accounts of the lives of the outlaws. See J.W. Walker, *The True History of Robin Hood* (Wakefield, 1952).

7. The section of the Great North Road between Ferrybridge and Doncaster was known as Watling Street (the name used in the ballad), in 1433. Kirklees, where Robin met his death, is only fifteen miles to the west.

8. Knight, *Robin Hood*, pp. 29–30. *The Paston Letters A.D. 1422–1509*, ed. J. Gairdner, 6 vols. (1904), v, p. 185.

9. J.C. Holt, *Robin Hood* (1989), p. 142. Knight, *Robin Hood*, p. 264.

10. Both Robin and Eustace ask their victims how much money they have and reward those who answer truthfully – but

whereas the monks' deceit repays the knight's honesty in the Geste there is no such parallel in *Wistasse*.

11. Holt, *Robin Hood*, pp. 73–4 & 88. St Mary's Church in Nottingham is named in the *Monk*, but this may owe more to Robin's well-attested devotion to Our Lady than to a real knowledge of the town.

12. Holt, *Robin Hood*, pp. 77–8. J.R. Maddicott, 'The birth and setting of the ballads of Robin Hood', *English Historical Review*, xciii (1978), p. 280.

13. Holt, *Robin Hood*, p. 79. Gerald of Wales, *The Journey Through Wales and The Description of Wales*, trans. L. Thorpe (Harmondsworth, 1987), p. 113.

14. The problem was that the Crown would have lost the right to charge an entry fine when the existing tenant-in-chief died and his son or another succeeded. The Church never 'died'.

15. Pollard, *Robin Hood*, p. 128. The privilege was renewed in 1309, and additional acquisitions were legitimized in 1315.

16. J.R. Maddicott points out that the unpublished Ancient Petitions in the National Archives record at least twenty-two complaints about the misbehaviour of fourteenth-century sheriffs, but only two such allegations were made against JPs. 'Birth and setting of the ballads of Robin Hood', p. 279.

3. THE ROBIN HOODS OF HISTORY

1. J.R. Maddicott comments that 'in view of the wealth of the English state archives and the quantities of information available on bandits such as the Folvilles and the Coterels, it seems very unlikely that a notorious outlaw called by that name could have escaped all notice in the records. It may be

that Robin Hood was one among several names for the same real figure'. 'The birth and setting of the ballads of Robin Hood', *English Historical Review*, xciii (1978), p. 297.

2. For the Cirencester Robin see J.C. Holt, *Robin Hood* (1989), p. 54. Robin of Burntoft is noticed by Professor Pollard, *Imagining Robin Hood* (2007), p. 15.

3. The expression was still in use in 1381. John Ball, one of the leaders of the Peasants' Revolt, or Great Rebellion, urged his followers to 'biddeth Piers Plowman go to his work, and chastise well Hobbe the Robbere'. S. Knight, *Robin Hood. A Complete Study of the English Outlaw* (1994), p. 263.

4. These paragraphs are based on Holt, *Robin Hood*, pp. 52 & 187–90.

5. A grave was originally a steward, and later, one of a number of administrative officials in townships in certain parts of Yorkshire and Lincolnshire.

6. This paragraph is based on J. Bellamy, *Robin Hood. an historical inquiry* (1985), pp. 114–6.

7. J.W. Walker, 'Robin Hood Identified', *Yorkshire Archaeological Journal*, xxxvi (1944–7), and *The True History of Robin Hood* (Wakefield, 1952).

8. Holt, *Robin Hood*, pp. 47–8.

9. Bellamy, *Robin Hood*, p. 39.

10. N. Fryde, *The tyranny and fall of Edward II 1321–1326* (Cambridge 1979), on which these paragraphs are based. Fryde notes the case of Constance Halliday who had fifteen children and whose late husband was owed £26 13s 4d by Earl Thomas. She petitioned the King but received nothing.

11. Rob Lynley and David Pilling have discovered a number of references in the National Archives to a Robert of Loxley

who held property in Huntingdon and who prosecuted landed disputes in several courts (including Nottingham), in the 1240s. The Loxley – Huntingdon – Nottingham connection is interesting, but there is nothing to suggest that he was ever known as Robin Hood or became an outlaw. Coincidence is probably at work again. See www.robinhoodloxley.net/mycustompage0002.htm

12. Holt, *Robin Hood*, p. 40.

13. Stephen Knight suggests that Bower may have been influenced by the fact that the victor of Evesham was Prince Edward, who, as Edward I, would 'hammer' the Scots. *Robin Hood*, p. 36.

14. J.M. Luxford, 'An English Chronicle entry on Robin Hood', *Journal of Medieval History*, vol. 35 (2009). Dr Luxford notes that there is no direct evidence that Robin and Wallace were associated in the late Middle Ages.

4. Friends, Foes & Gravestones

1. The same is true of a Little John de Cockroft of Sowerby who appears in the Rolls in 1324. A Robert Little is mentioned in 1275, but this proves only that the surname was in use in the area at that date. 'Nailer' may derive from Colonel Naylor, see p. 80.

2. J.C. Holt, *Robin Hood* (1989), p. 188.

3. J.G. Bellamy, *Robin Hood. an historical inquiry* (1985), pp. 122–4.

4. Although Much is one of the principal characters in the *Monk*, Will is only mentioned briefly.

5. See R.B. Dobson & J. Taylor, *Rymes of Robyn Hood. An Introduction to the English Outlaw* (Gloucester, 1989), pp.

79, 80, 100, 108.

6. I am grateful to Dr B.M.M. Brown for his advice on this point.

7. P. Valentine Harris, *The Truth About Robin Hood* (Mansfield, 1973), pp. 73–5.

8. Bellamy, *Robin Hood*, pp. 99–105.

9. Although not everyone agrees. Professor Bellamy notes that there is a Wiresdale near Great Edston, a Wyverdale in Helperthorpe, and a Wyveresdesley near Bingley, all in Yorkshire. None of these are close to Barnsdale, however, and other possibilities are Lyvereshale (modern Loversall), just south of Doncaster, and an ancient fort called Iverishagh, near Oxton, nine miles north-east of Nottingham, which was just within the bounds of Sherwood in the early thirteenth century. The valley of the River Erewash between Nottinghamshire and Derbyshire was known as Irewysdale, and the Erewash, which rises on the eastern edge of Sherwood, ran only two and a half miles from the motte and bailey castle at Annesley (Nottinghamshire). Bellamy, *Robin Hood*, pp. 78–80.

10. Holt, *Robin Hood*, p. 59.

11. Geoffrey Chaucer, *The Canterbury Tales*, ed. T. Tyrwhitt (1867), pp. 9–10.

12. A pinder, or pinner, was a pound keeper, whose job it was to impound all stray cattle. In the story he fights Robin, Little John and Will before giving them food and drink and agreeing to join the outlaw band.

13. Faucumberg's case is argued fully in Professor Bellamy's *Robin Hood*, pp. 45–56.

14. For Oxenford, see J.R. Maddicott, 'The birth and setting of the ballads of Robin Hood', *English Historical Review*, xciii (1978), pp. 286–93. The Exchequer was based at York

between May 1333 and September 1338.

15. This Roger may not have been the prioress's lover, but he was accused of adultery with Agnes, the wife of Philip de Pavely, in 1309. Bellamy, *Robin Hood*, p. 120.

16. M.H. Keen, *The Outlaws of Medieval Legend* (1961), p. 180, quoting Richard Grafton, *Chronicle at Large* (1569), p. 85.

17. Opinion as expressed by Richard Gough, *Sepulchral Monuments of Great Britain* (1786), p. cviii.

18. Quoted by Holt, *Robin Hood*, p. 42, and Keen, *Outlaws*, p. 181.

19. The kalends, or calends, was the first day of the month in the Roman calendar.

20. Dobson & Taylor, *Rymes of Robyn Hood*, p. 301.

21. J. Brome, *An Historical Account of Mr Roger's Travels* (1694), pp. 90–1, quoted by Holt, *Robin Hood*, p. 178.

22. R. Thoroton, *Antiquities of Nottinghamshire*, ed. J. Throsby (1797), ii, pp. 170–1, quoted by Holt, *Robin Hood*, p. 178.

23. Quoted by G. Phillips & M. Keatman, *Robin Hood. The Man Behind the Myth* (1995), p. 44.

24. BL, Cotton Julius BXII, fols 9ᵛ – 10ʳ, quoted by E. Cavell, 'Henry VII, the north of England and the first provincial progress of 1486', *Northern History*, 39 (Sept 2002), p. 193.

25. A.J. Pollard, *Imagining Robin Hood*, (2004), p. 70.

26. J.W. Walker, *The True History of Robin Hood* (Wakefield, 1952), pp. 129–32. Walker attributes the story to Miss Frances Stanhope who heard it from an old woodman, the sexton's son. Thomas Gent (*c.*1730) tells a similar story of how an unnamed knight converted Robin's grave slab into a hearth stone, but quickly returned it when it refused to remain in place!

27. A coat of mail would have been an expensive item, and John is unlikely to have owned one unless he had taken it from a

higher born victim.

28. Walker, *Robin Hood*, p. 131. In 1992 the then curator of Cannon Hall museum expressed the hope that the bow and other exhibits removed when the house was purchased by Barnsley Corporation would be returned to them, but the situation remained unchanged in 2009 and the bow's present whereabouts are unknown. I am grateful to Jane Galvin of Barnsley Metropolitan Borough Council for confirming this.

29. Quoted by Maurice Keen in *Outlaws*, p. 182. Boece said that people of his generation were smaller because 'they were made effeminate with lust and intemperance of mouth'.

30. A. Mee, *The King's England. Nottinghamshire* (1938), p. 40.

5. 'BAD' KINGS...

1. Richard had been betrothed to Philip Augustus's sister Alice since childhood, but his feisty mother Eleanor of Aquitaine determined his marriage to Berengaria, even escorting the bride to Sicily personally. Evidence that Richard was homosexual is decidedly thin on the ground.

2. The Emperor's principal opponent was Henry the Lion, Duke of Saxony and Bavaria, husband of Richard's sister Matilda.

3. Normally, the estates of a father who lacked sons would have been divided equally among his daughters, but Henry II's new theory was that married daughters had already received their allotted portions, and an unmarried sister (in this case Isabella), was entitled to the rest.

4. Roger of Howden.

5. John had had no children by Isabella of Gloucester after

ten years of marriage, and 'divorced' her in 1199 on the grounds that, as second cousins, their marriage fell within the prohibited degrees.

6. This is Matthew Paris's version written fifty years later. It is worth noting that although Philip taunted John with Arthur's death he did not exploit the obvious propaganda value of an undoubted murder, and that Eleanor, Arthur's sister, was treated kindly by her uncle – she lived until 1241.

6. .... AND 'GOOD' OUTLAWS

1. E.L.G. Stones, 'The Folvilles of Ashby-Folville, Leicestershire and their Associates in Crime', *Transactions of the Royal Historical Society,* 5th series, vii (1957), p. 131.

2. *Ibid.,* pp. 117-36. J.G. Bellamy, 'The Coterel Gang: an Anatomy of a Band of Fourteenth-century Criminals', *English Historical Review,* lxxix (1964), pp. 698–717.

3. Professor Stones points out that the literal sense of the papal letter is that Richard's accomplices were also beheaded, and these may have included some of his brothers. 'The Folvilles', p. 130.

4. *Ibid.,* p. 129.

5. *Ibid.,* p. 124.

6. J. R. Maddicott, 'The birth and setting of the ballads of Robin Hood', *English Historical Review,* xciii (1978), p. 295.

7. Stones, 'The Folvilles', p. 133.

8. 'Setting a thief to catch a thief' was by no means unusual at this period.

9. Bellamy, 'The Coterel Gang', p. 702.

10. *Calendar of the Patent Rolls 1334–1338* (1895), p. 372, quoted in Bellamy, *The Coterel Gang,* p. 712.

11. A.J. Pollard, *Imagining Robin Hood* (2004), p. 93.

12. *Ibid.*, p. 92.

13. William Langland, *The Vision of Piers Plowman*, ed. A.V.C. Schmidt (Everyman, 1995), pp. 335–6.

14. Maddicott, 'Robin Hood', p. 297.

15. Pollard, *Robin Hood*, p. 109.

16. M.H. Keen, *The Outlaws of Medieval Legend* (1961), p. 93.

17. J.G. Bellamy, *Crime and Public Order in England in the Later Middle Ages* (1973), p. 88.

18. *Ibid.*, p. 30.

7. Henry III & Simon de Montfort

1. Professor Carpenter believes that 'it was not part of his [Henry's] policy to surround himself with foreign relatives to the exclusion of English nobles', but accepts that 'it is true that in the 1240s and 1250s the first place at court was often enjoyed by the queen's Savoyard uncles and the king's Lusignan half-brothers'. There were surely some English barons who would have played a larger role in government in other circumstances, and who were disappointed that they did not. D.A. Carpenter, *The Reign of Henry III* (1996), p. 93.

2. The inheritance was partitioned in 1207. Simon the elder became nominally entitled to the 'Honour of Leicester' based on the Leicester properties; the other half, known as the 'Honour of Winchester', or Winton, went to his aunt Margaret and her husband, the Earl of Winchester Saer de Quincy.

3. Much as her sibling Isabella had been married to the Emperor Frederick II in 1235.

4. As remembered by the chronicler Rishanger, quoted by J.R.

Maddicott, *Simon de Montfort* (Cambridge, 1994), p. 9.

5. At least on paper – in practice it was never easy to collect the dower from the numerous Marshal heirs.

6. *English Historical Documents*, vol. III, 1189–1327, ed. H. Rothwell (1975), pp. 359–60.

7. Quoted in F.M. Powicke, *The Thirteenth Century 1216–1307* (Oxford, 1962), p. 121.

8. Louis may also have changed his mind after the Savoyards and other aliens who had been mistreated and expelled during the 'first war of the barons', had portrayed the reform movement in the worst possible light.

8. The Unlikely Saint

1. C.H. Knowles, *Simon de Montfort 1265–1965* (1965), p. 26, to whose excellent booklet I am indebted for the thoughts in these paragraphs. Guy, one of Simon's younger sons, subsequently murdered Henry of Almain (Henry III's nephew), to 'avenge' his father's death.

2. F.M. Powicke, *King Henry III and the Lord Edward* (2 vols., Oxford 1947), pp. 509–10, on which these paragraphs are also based. See also Michael Wood, *In Search of England* (2000), chapter 13.

3. *English Historical Documents*, vol. 3, 1189–1327, ed. H. Rothwell (1975), pp. 916–7. See also the version in *The Political Songs of England, from the Reign of John to that of Edward II*, ed. & trans. T. Wright (Camden Society, 1839), pp. 125–7. Songs were being written in praise of de Montfort even in his lifetime, see *The Chronicle of William de Rishanger of the Barons' Wars. The Miracles of Simon de Montfort*, ed. J.O.

Halliwell (Camden Society, 1840), pp. 19–20.

4. William fitzStephen and others. *The Life of Thomas Becket, Chancellor and Archbishop*, trans. & ed. G. Greenaway (1961), p. 159.

5. F. Barlow, *Thomas Becket* (2000), p. 250.

6. *English Historical Documents*, p. 382.

7. What we do not know, of course, is how many people who appealed to Earl Simon did *not* have their requests granted. This might put the number in better perspective.

8. All 212 miracles have been printed (in Latin) in *The Miracles of Simon de Montfort*, pp. 67–110. This selection is taken from W.H. Rippin, *Simon de Montfort, Earl of Leicester* (Leicester, 1919), pp. 63–4, G.W. Prothero, *The Life of Simon de Montfort* (1877), pp. 371–3, and J.R. Maddicott, *Simon de Montfort* (Cambridge, 1994), p. 346.

9. *Rishanger's Chronicle*, p. 71, translated from the Latin.

10. These figures have been calculated by D.C. Cox, *The Battle of Evesham. A New Account* (Evesham, 1988), pp. 21–2.

11. *Annales Monastici*, ed. H.R. Luard, 5 vols. (1864–9), iv, p.177. *Annales Monasterii de Osenia A.D. 1016–1347*.The *Annales* place this in 1265, which is rather surprising in view of the subsequent veneration of the tomb. However, there are other examples of an original site continuing to attract pilgrims even after the remains had been translated elsewhere.

12. J.C. Holt, *Robin Hood* (1989), p. 112.

13. *Calendar of Inquisitions Miscellaneous (Chancery)*, II, Edward II & 1–22 Edward III, 1307–1349 (1916), no. 2103, pp. 528–9.

14. The painting, which dates from *c.*1340, was commissioned by the local Giffard family whose members had supported Earl Thomas.

9. THE DISINHERITED

1. The value of land in 1266 was reckoned as ten times its annual revenue. Thus those who had fought for Earl Simon were fined five years' income or half the market value (a few who had given particular offence suffered the maximum seven years' penalty); those who had not fought themselves but who had persuaded others to do so or to withhold their support from the King were to pay the equivalent of two years' revenue; men who had been caught up in the movement unwillingly and had abandoned it as soon as they could were penalized to the tune of a year's income; and those who had taken refuge in Northampton's churches instead of resisting the baronial takeover were to pay half a year's revenue or a twentieth of the value of their properties. Landless knights and men-at-arms were to lose a third of their goods.

2. A.J. Pollard, *Imagining Robin Hood* (2004), pp. 195–6. John d'Eyvill was given permission to fortify his house at Hode, or Hood (Yorkshire) in 1264, and it has been suggested that he and his brother Robert (a dispossessed knight and yeoman) may have been 'role-models for characters portrayed in the rhymes'. See O. De Ville, 'The Deyvilles and the Genesis of the Robin Hood Legend', *Nottingham Medieval Studies,* xliii (1999).

3. See C.H. Knowles, 'The Resettlement of England after the Barons War, 1264–67', *Transactions of the Royal Historical Society,* 5th series, 32 (1982), pp. 34–5.

4. J.R. Maddicott, *Simon de Montfort* (Cambridge, 1994), p. 322.

5. His lands were valued at 2,000 marks per annum (£1,333) when he became a royal ward on the death of his father in 1254.

6. National.Archives, *Coram Rege Rolls*, 2–3 Edward I, roll 11, m. 6. The case is well summarized in G.E.C., et al., *The Complete Peerage*, 12 vols. (1910–59), iv, pp. 200–1.

7. Edward had given Elham to Leyburn as a reward for his good service, but the gift was subsequently held to be contrary to the terms of the King's grant of the manor to his son. Leyburn was accused of misappropriating the income, and broke with Edward when he was ordered to refund £1,820 from the proceeds of his other lands. See Kathryn Faulkner's summary of his life in the *Oxford Dictionary of National Biography*, ed. H.C.G. Matthew & B. Harrison, 60 vols. (Oxford, 2004), 33, pp. 695–6.

8. Quoted by Alun Lewis, 'Roger Leyburn and the Pacification of England, 1265–7', *English Historical Review*, ccxiv (1939), p. 195, on which this summary is based.

9. *Calendar of the Patent Rolls, Henry III 1258–1266* (1910), p. 636.

10. *Complete* Peerage, iv, p. 197 & xii, pp. 753–4. *Oxford DNB*, 33, pp. 695–6. Eleanor Ferrers was Robert's sister and her parents' seventh daughter.

11. Knowles 'Resettlement of England', p. 38.

10. ROGER GODBERD & WALTER DEVYAS

1. Like, for example, the fifteenth-century Pastons, who had a distinct preference for the name 'John' and who indisputably made their own luck.

2. G.F. Farnham, *Leicestershire Medieval Village Notes*, 6 vols. (Leicester 1928–33), iv, p. 190. One writer claims that Roger died in 1293 and that his son 'fought off a challenge to

be known as the village squire', but I have been unable to locate his source. B. Benison, *Robin Hood. The Real Story* (Mansfield, 2004).

3. G.F. Farnham, *Leicestershire Medieval Pedigrees* (Leicester, 1925), p. 119. *Report on the Manuscripts of the late Reginald Rawdon Hastings of The Manor House, Ashby de la Zouch,* Historical Manuscripts Commission, 78, vol. 1 (1928), pp. 29 & 31. Henry E. Huntington Library, HAD 1954. I am grateful to Mary L. Robertson, Chief Curator of Manuscripts at the Huntington, for checking the originals for me.

4. *Hastings Manuscripts Report*, p. 38, where the younger Roger witnessed a grant of land.

5. I am grateful to Lesley Boatwright for interpreting the abbreviated and somewhat garbled Latin and providing the translation.

6. Farnham, *Leics Medieval Village Notes*, iv., p. 190. The case was still before the courts in 1262–3 when Jordan asked that Roger should be compelled to honour the agreement, but with, it seems, no greater success. Roger again failed to appear, and the sheriff was ordered to take all his lands, tenements and chattels into the King's hands 'and to keep them safely so that he answers for the issues'. The final outcome is unknown. *The 1263 Surrey Eyre*, ed. S. Stewart, (Surrey Record Society, 2006), xl, p. 183.

7. *Calendar of the Patent Rolls, Henry III 1258–1266* (1910), pp. 395–6.

8. Robert Ferrers absented himself from the battle of Lewes, and it would be reasonable to assume that Godberd did the same.

9. *Calendar of the Close Rolls, Henry III, 1264–1268* (1937), p. 353.

10. *Calendar of the Patent Rolls, Henry III 1266–1272* (1913), pp. 7 & 11.

11. *Ibid.*, p. 16.

12. A. Lewis, 'Roger Leyburn and the Pacification of England, 1265–7', *English Historical Review*, ccxiv (1939), pp. 208–9. See also J.C. Holt, *Robin Hood* (1989), p. 97.

13. TNA JUST 1/1222. I am grateful to Lesley Boatwright for locating and transcribing this document for me.

14. *Cal. Pat. Rolls, 1266–1272*, p. 622. It is worth comparing the document quoted in Appendix 2 with its counterpart providing for a loan from the merchants: 'Whereas lately on complaint by the prelates, magnates and nobles of the realm the king was informed that through outlaws, robbers, thieves and malefactors, mounted and on foot, in the counties of Nottingham, Leicester and Derby, wandering by day and night, so many and great homicides and robberies were done that no one with a small company could pass through those parts without being taken and killed or spoiled of his goods, the king provided by his council that 100 marks should be received as a loan from Florentine merchants to the use of Reynold de Grey, etc.' *Ibid.*, pp. 633–4

15. J.C. Holt, *Robin Hood* (1989), p. 98, where no reference is given.

16. *Cal. Pat. Rolls 1266–72*, p. 320.

17. *Ibid.*, p. 578.

18. *Calendar of the Close Rolls, Henry III, 1268–1272* (1938), p. 462.

19. *Ibid.*, *Cal. Pat. Rolls 1266–72*, p. 320.

20. D. Crook, 'Jordan Castle and the Foliot Family of Grimston, 1225–1330', *Transactions of the Thoroton Society*, vol. 112 (2008), pp. 151–2.

21. *Calendar of Inquisitions Miscellaneous (Chancery)*, I, Henry III & Edward I, 1219–1307 (1916), p. 293. Lestrange himself claimed 100 marks (£66 13s 4d) for expenses incurred in his pursuit and capture of Devyas. *Cal. Close Rolls 1268–1272*, p. 584.

22. *Chronicles of the Reigns of Stephen, Henry II and Richard I, ii., A Continuation of William of Newburgh's History to AD. 1298*, ed. R. Howlett (Rolls Series, 1885). p. 563

23. *Rotuli Hundredorum Temp. Hen. III. & Edw. I. in Turr' Lond'*, 2 vols. (1812, 1818), ii, p. 312.

24. *Cal. Pat. Rolls 1266–1272*, p. 698. TNA JUST 1/1222.

25. The Forty-Seventh Annual Report of the Deputy Keeper of the Public Records (1886), p. 343.

26. *Calendar of the Patent Rolls, Edward I, 1272–1281* (1901), pp. 123–4.

27. Reginald Grey was summoned to Parliament as the first Lord Grey of Wilton (Herefordshire) in 1290 or 1295, while John and Lucy's son Henry became the first Lord Grey of Codnor (Derbyshire) in 1299. G.E.C., et al., *The Complete Peerage*, 12 vols. (1910–59), vi, pp. 123 & 171–2.

28. Thomas Huchun's mother subsequently accused the abbot of 'instigating' the attack. *Cal. Pat. Rolls 1272–1281*, p. 123.

29. Nichols, the historian of Leicestershire, notes that William Talbot, son of Adam Talbot, was lord of the manor of Swanington in 1278, but it would be unwise to assume that this was because Godberd was unavoidably absent. J. Nichols, *The History and Antiquities of the County of Leicester*, 4 vols. (1795–1811), iii, p. 1122.

30. *The Sherwood Forest Book*, ed. H. E. Boulton, Thoroton Society xxiii (1964), pp. 108–82, especially, pp. 128–30. A significant number of those convicted had – not surprisingly

– died prior to the eyre being held, but Roger and Geoffrey were clearly still alive.

31. Helen Boulton refers to 'the small number of persons [convicted] from whom any money was then apparently forthcoming'. *Sherwood Forest Book*, p. 109.

32. An effigy in the church at Ashby Folville (Leics.), has been identified as Eustace de Folville. A piece of iron protruding from the figure's chest is said to represent the point of a lance with which he was killed by a neighbour, but is more probably an attachment for a now lost shield.

11. The Real Robin Hood

1. *The Sherwood Forest Book*, ed. H.E. Boulton, Thoroton Society, xxiii (1964), p. 128. 'xxvi cervos et xlv bissas et xliii damos et lxvii damas'.

2. in fytte three of the *Geste.*

3. *Calendar of the Patent Rolls, Henry III 1266–1272* (1913), pp. 622 & 633–4.

4. *Ibid.,* p. 622.

5. *Calendar of the Charter Rolls 1226–1257* (1903), p. 375.

6. J.C. Holt, *Robin Hood* (1989), p. 99.

7. T. Molyneux-Smith, *Robin Hood and the Lords of Wellow* (Nottinghamshire County Council 1998), p. 17.

8. *Calendar of the Patent Rolls, Henry III 1258–1266* (1910), p. 301. *Cal Pat. Rolls 1266–1272*, p. 65.

9. *Cal. Pat. Rolls 1266–1272*, p. 320.

10. Holt, *Robin Hood*, p. 40.

11. F.J. Child, *English and Scottish Ballads*, v. (1858) pp. xi–xii.

12. A.J. Pollard, *Imagining Robin Hood* (2004), p. 36.

Appendix 1: Gamelyn & Adam Bell

1. M. Keen, *The Outlaws of Medieval Legend* (1961), p. 79.
2. It is a curious comment on the morality of the era that Adam, Gamelyn's ally, tells him to be careful not to shed the clerics' blood, but breaking their legs is fine!
3. J.C. Holt, *Robin Hood* (1989), pp. 66–71.

Appendix 2: Selected Documents

1. Presumably this is St Stephen the martyr. There was another St Stephen whose day fell on 2 August.
2. *latro* = robber, one who has committed *latrocinium*, larceny.
3. This is a literal translation. It means 'he asks for a trial by the juries of the aforesaid counties'.

BIBLIOGRAPHY

The place of publication is London unless otherwise stated:

Annales Monastici, ed. H.R. Luard, 5 vols. (1864–9). *Annales Monasterii de Osenia A.D. 1016–1347*.

Barlow, F., *Thomas Becket* (2000).

Bellamy, J. G., *Crime and Public Order in England in the Later Middle Ages* (1973).

Bellamy, J.G., *Robin Hood, an historical enquiry* (1985).

Bellamy, J.G., 'The Coterel Gang: an Anatomy of a Band of Fourteenth-century Criminals', *English Historical Review*, lxxix (1964).

Blamires, D., *Robin Hood: A Hero For All Times*, John Rylands Library Exhibition Guide (1998).

Walter Bower, *Scotichronicon*, ed. D.E.R. Watt, 9 vols., (Aberdeen, 1987–98).

Calendar of the Charter Rolls, Henry III, 1226–1257 (1903).

Calendar of the Close Rolls, Henry III, 1264–1268 (1937), *1268–1272* (1938).

Calendar of Inquisitions Miscellaneous (Chancery), i, Henry III & Edward I, 1219–1307 (1916). ii. Edward II & 1–22 Edward III, 1307–1349 (1916).

Calendar of the Patent Rolls, Henry III 1258–1266 (1910), *1266–1272* (1913), Edward I *1272–1281* (1901).

Carpenter, D.A., *The Reign of Henry III* (1996).

Cavell, E., 'Henry VII, the north of England and the first provincial progress of 1486', *Northern History*, 39 (Sept., 2002).

Child, F.J., *The English and Scottish Popular Ballads*, 5 vols. in 3 (1956).

Chronicles of the Reigns of Stephen, Henry II and Richard I, ii., *A Continuation of William of Newburgh's History to A.D. 1298*, ed. R. Howlett (Rolls Series, 1885).

Cox, D.C., *The Battle of Evesham, A New Account* (1998).

Crook, D., 'Jordan Castle and the Foliot Family of Grimston, 1225–1330', *Transactions of the Thoroton Society*, vol. 112 (2008).

Crook, D., 'Some further evidence concerning the dating of the origins of the legend of Robin Hood', *English Historical Review*, 99 (1984).

Crook, D., 'The Sheriff of Nottingham and Robin Hood: The Genesis of the Legend?' *Thirteenth Century England II*, ed. P.R. Coss and S.D. Lloyd, (Woodbridge, 1988).

De Ville, O., 'The Deyvilles and the Genesis of the Robin Hood Legend', *Nottingham Medieval Studies*, xliii (1999).

Dobson, R.B., & Taylor, J., 'Robin Hood of Barnsdale: A Fellow Thou Has Long Sought', *Northern History*, xxix (1983).

Dobson, R.B., *Rymes of Robyn Hood. An Introduction to the English Outlaw* (Gloucester, 1989).

English Historical Documents, vol 3, 1189–1327, ed. H. Rothwell (1975).

Excerpta è Rotulis Finium in Turri Londinensi asservatis, Henrico tertio rege, 2 vols. (Record Commission, 1835–6).

Farnham, G.F., *Leicestershire Medieval Pedigrees* (Leicester, 1925).

Farnham, G.F., *Leicestershire Medieval Village Notes*, 6 vols. (Leicester 1928–33).

Finucane, R.C., *Miracles and Pilgrims. Popular Beliefs in Medieval England* (New York, 1995).

William fitzStephen and others. *The Life of Thomas Becket, Chancellor and Archbishop*, trans. & ed. G. Greenaway (1961).

Forty-seventh annual report of the Deputy Keeper of the Public Records (1886).

Fryde, N., *The tyranny and fall of Edward II 1321–1326* (Cambridge, 1979).

G.E.C., et al., *The Complete Peerage*, 12 vols. (1910–59).

Gerald of Wales, *The Journey Through Wales and The Description of Wales*, trans. L. Thorpe (Harmondsworth, 1987).

Harris, P.V., *The Truth About Robin Hood* (Mansfield, 1973).

Holt, J.C., *Robin Hood* (1989).

Holt, J.C., 'The Origins and Audience of the Ballads of Robin Hood', *Past and Present*, 18 (1960).

The Huntington Library, HAD 1954, 1959.

Keen, M., *The Outlaws of Medieval Legend* (1961).

Knight, S., *Robin Hood. A Complete Study of the English Outlaw* (1994).

Knowles, C.H., *Simon de Montfort 1265–1965* (1965).

Knowles, C.H., 'The Resettlement of England after the Barons War, 1264–67', *Transactions of the Royal Historical Society*, 5th series, 32 (1982).

William Langland, *The Vision of Piers Plowman*, ed. A.V.C. Schmidt (Everyman, 1995).

Lewis, A., 'Roger Leyburn and the Pacification of England, 1265–

7', *English Historical Review*, ccxiv (1939).

Luxford, J.M., 'An English Chronicle entry on Robin Hood', *Journal of Medieval History,* vol. 35 (2009).

Maddicott, J.R., 'The birth and setting of the ballads of Robin Hood', *English Historical Review,* xciii (1978).

Maddicott, J.R., *Thomas of Lancaster* (Oxford, 1970).

Maddicott, J.R., *Simon de Montfort* (Cambridge, 1994).

McFarlane, K.B., 'Had Edward I a 'Policy' Towards the Earls', *The Nobility of Medieval England* (Oxford, 1973).

Mee, A., *The King's England. Nottinghamshire* (1938).

Molyneux-Smith, T., *Robin Hood and the Lords of Wellow* (Nottinghamshire County Council 1998).

Nichols, J., *The History and Antiquities of the County of Leicester,* 4 vols. (1795–1811).

Oxford Dictionary of National Biography, ed. H.C.G. Matthew & B. Harrison, 60 vols. (Oxford, 2004).

The Paston Letters A.D. 1422–1509, ed. J. Gairdner, 6 vols. (1904).

Phillips, G., & Keatman, M., *Robin Hood. The Man Behind the Myth* (1995).

(The) Political Songs of England, from the Reign of John to that of Edward II, ed. & trans. T. Wright (Camden Society, 1839).

Pollard, A.J., *Imagining Robin Hood* (2004).

Powicke, F.M., *King Henry III and the Lord Edward,* 2 vols. (Oxford, 1947).

Powicke, F.M., *The Thirteenth Century 1216–1307* (Oxford, 1962).

Prothero, G.W., *The Life of Simon de Montfort* (1877).

Report on the Manuscripts of the late Reginald Rawdon Hastings of The Manor House, Ashby de la Zouch, Historical Manuscripts

Commission, 78, vol. 1 (1928).

Rippin, W.H., *Simon de Montfort, Earl of Leicester* (Leicester, 1919).

(Rishanger). *The Chronicle of William de Rishanger of the Barons' Wars. The Miracles of Simon de Montfort*, ed. J.O. Halliwell (Camden Society, 1840).

Ritson, J., *Robin Hood. A Collection of all the Ancient Poems, Songs and Ballads, now extant, Relative to the Celebrated English Outlaw*, 2 vols. (1887).

Rotuli Hundredorum Temp. Hen. III. & Edw. I. in Turr' Lond', 2 vols, (1812, 1818).

The National Archives, JUST 1/1222.

The Sherwood Forest Book, ed. H.E. Boulton, Thoroton Society, xxiii (1964).

Stones, E.L.G., 'The Folvilles of Ashby-Folville, Leicestershire and their Associates in Crime', *Transactions of the Royal Historical Society*, 5th series, vii (1957).

The 1263 Surrey Eyre, ed. S. Stewart, Surrey Record Society, xl (2006).

Walker, J.W., *The True History of Robin Hood* (Wakefield, 1952).

Walker, J.W., 'Robin Hood Identified', *Yorkshire Archaeological Journal*, xxxvi (1944–7).

Wood, M., *In Search of England* (2000).

LIST OF ILLUSTRATIONS

1. Robin Hood's statue, Castle Green, Nottingham, by James Woodford. Ironically, the robber is sometimes robbed of his arrow and even the lower half of his bow. Author's collection.

2. 'Robyn hod in scherewod stod'. Statue of the outlaw at the Sherwood Forest Visitor Centre. Author's collection.

3. The Major Oak, Sherwood Forest, named after a Major Rooke who lived locally in the eighteenth century. Robin and his 'merry men' are said to have met beneath its branches. Author's collection.

4. Robin Hood's Well beside the old Great North Road south of Barnsdale. The arched shelter was erected by the Earl of Carlisle before 1730. Author's collection.

5. St Mary's Church Edwinstowe (Nottinghamshire), where tradition says that Robin and Maid Marian were married. Author's collection.

6. & 7. Little John's Grave at St Michael's church, Hathersage (Derbyshire), is nearly 14 foot long and is maintained by the Ancient Order of Foresters. The older stone, with its distinctive 'L I' (Little Ihon) is in the church porch. Author's collection.

8. 'Little John's Well', on the Longshaw Estate (National Trust), near Sheffield. One of several local features associated with the outlaws. Author's collection.

9. Some stones in the churchyard of St Mary of the Purfication, Blidworth (Nottinghamshire), said to mark the place where Will Scarlett was buried. They probably formed part of the tower of the old (now demolished) church. Author's collection.

10. & 11. The apse and south doorway of the Norman chapel at Steetley (Nottinghamshire), where tradition says that Alan a Dale was married and Friar Tuck brought Robin and his men to prayers. Both author's collection.

12. St Mary's Church, Gisburn (Gisborne), Lancashire, presumed home of Sir Guy. The building has changed little since the thirteenth century. Author's collection.

13. 'Ye Olde Trip to Jerusalem' inn, Nottingham, dating from c. 1189. The name recalls the era of the Crusades. Author's collection.

14. The remains of 'King John's Palace' at Clipstone (Nottinghamshire), a twelfth-century hunting lodge in the forest. Author's collection.

15. Peveril Castle (Derbyshire), built by Henry II, was the administrative centre of the 'Forest of the Peak'. Author's collection.

16. Simon de Montfort, a portrait in the west window of the Lichfield chapel in All Saints Church, Evesham (Worcestershire), installed in 1883. Author's collection.

17. Granite cross memorial to de Montfort, erected at the expense of Canon Walker, the then vicar, and unveiled by Lord Swinfen, Master of the Rolls, in 1919. The twelfth-century churches of

30. Henry III, the King opposed by Simon de Montfort, whose troubled reign may have given rise to the Robin Hood stories. © Jonathan Reeve JR1248b12p324 12001300.

31. A thirteenth-century drawing of London from the margin of a manuscript of Geoffrey of Monmouth's *History of the Kings of Britain*. London dwarfed all other cities in the kingdom, and control of it was critical to any political cause. © Jonathan Reeve JR350b18p159COL 12001300.

32. A self-portrait of Geoffrey Chaucer. Chaucer was one of the first to allude to Robin Hood, without specifically naming him, in his *Troilus and Criseyde* (1380). © Jonathan Reeve JR991b1p2 13001400.

33. Magna Carta, the great charter of liberties that King John granted his subjects at Runnymede in June 1215. Autocratic kings like Henry III could not ignore it, and it became the foundation stone of all later attempts at reform. © Jonathan Reeve JR810b11fp241 12001250.

34. Robin competing in an archery contest, a theme included in three of the four earliest surviving ballads, *Robin Hood and the Potter, Robin Hood and Guy of Gisborne*, and a *Little Geste of Robyn Hode and his Meiny* (followers). © Jonathan Reeve JR1264b72fp192 12001300.

35. Robin and his men move cautiously through the forest. These Victorian prints are inevitably stereotyped, but this one captures the danger of the outlaw life and the ever-present fear of discovery and arrest. © Jonathan Reeve JR1388b77fc 12001300.

36. Robin and his 'Merry Men' as they are usually portrayed in films and popular literature – relaxed, carefree, and with plenty of time to discover which of them is the best shot! ©

Jonathan Reeve JR1371b75fpi 12001300.

37. A lady, her son, and an abbot ride through the forest. They were aware of the danger of ambush – hence the guards – but had little choice but to pass through high-risk areas when the path took them that way. © Jonathan Reeve JR1390b77fp18 12001300.

38. Robin, disguised as a potter, gives the last of his borrowed pots to the sheriff's wife. It was a popular story-line found in tales told of other outlaws, notably Hereward the Wake and Eustace the Monk. © Jonathan Reeve JR1374b76fp64 12001300.

39. Friar Tuck was a real person, at least in the sense that Robert Stafford, a chaplain of Linfield, in Sussex, borrowed or coined the name when he led an outlaw band in the early fifteenth century. In *Robin Hood and the Curtal Friar,* he is obliged to carry Robin across a river. © Jonathan Reeve JR1376b76fp120 12001300.

40. Robin agrees to help a poor knight who is journeying to York to plead with the abbot of St Mary's for more time to repay his debt, and allows Little John to act as his squire. A story from the *Geste.* © Jonathan Reeve JR1379b76fp200 12001300.

41. A monk of St Mary's abbey is captured by the outlaws and is found to have exactly double the amount owed by the knight is his possession. He is relieved of his money and the story ends happily – for Robin and the knight! © Jonathan Reeve JR1381b76fp256 12001300.

42. The king of the ballads is always chivalrous and ready to forgive when the situation is explained to him, but most rulers would have been more inclined to hang Robin and his men than pardon them. Here, he reveals himself to the outlaws in a scene from the *Geste.* © Jonathan Reeve JR1383b76fp296 12001300.

43. The abbess of Kirklees deceitfully lures an apprehensive Robin

to his death. Robin had asked her to bleed him to cure his sickness, and had dismissed warnings that she was up to no good. © Jonathan Reeve JR1387b76fp352 12001300.

44. Robin Hood as he is often seen in childrens' books, wearing clothes that are two or three centuries too late for the real Robin. Barry Vincent, after Louis Read by kind permission of Keith Branigan, University of Sheffield.

45. An old story-teller and a young listener, an engraving by Thomas Berwick, c. 1795, from J. Ritson, *Robin Hood: A Collection of all the Ancient Poems, Songs and Ballads, now extant, Relative to the Celebrated English Outlaw,* 2 vols. (1887). The stories may have been retold and revised on many occasions before the final (printed) versions emerged. Author's collection.

46. Robin Hood fighting Guy of Gisborne (Berwick in Ritson). Guy is Robin's bitterest enemy after the Sheriff of Nottingham, although we are never told why. Author's collection.

47 & 48. The dying Robin, supported by Little John, prepares to shoot an arrow indicating where he wants to be buried after his betrayal by the prioress and his battle with Sir Roger of Doncaster at Kirklees priory. Author's collection and © Jonathan Reeve JR1395b77fp360 12001300.

49. This picture, ostensibly of Robin, was printed on the front of the *Gest of Robyn Hode and his meyne, and the proud Sheryfe of Nottingham* published in 1508, but had been used to depict Chaucer's yeoman seventeen years before. Barry Vincent by kind permission of Keith Branigan, University of Sheffield

50. Archery practice at the butts, from the Lutterell Psalter, *c.*1340. Could the hooded figure who has just scored a bullseye be Robin himself? © Jonathan Reeve JR761b11p438 13001350.

51. The gatehouse of Kirklees priory, where Robin is said to have

been murdered, as it appeared in the nineteenth century. Barry Vincent, after Berwick by kind permission of Keith Branigan, University of Sheffield.

52. 'Robin Hood and his betrayer' (Berwick in Ritson). Robin allowed the prioress to bleed him for medicinal reasons, but she deliberately bled him to death. Author's collection.

53. Robin Hood's grave-slab at Kirklees, drawn by Nathaniel Johnson in 1665. From J.W. Walker, *The True History of Robin Hood* (Wakefield, 1952), author's collection.

54. Robin's grave at Kirklees as it would have appeared in the nineteenth century. Geoffrey Wheeler.

55. Robin Hood relics displayed at St Anne's Well, Nottingham, drawn by John Throsby (from R. Thoroton, *Antiquities of Nottingham* (1797). They include his cap, gravestone (compare with illustrations 20 and 53), and part of his chair. Author's Collection.

56. Little John's original gravestone (actually a grave-slab) at Hathersage, a drawing showing details now almost worn away (compare with illustration 7). (Barry Vincent)

57. Little John's Cottage at Hathersage, 1832. From J.W. Walker, *The True History of Robin Hood* (Wakefield, 1952), author's collection.

58. Richard I, the king most often associated with Robin Hood. © Jonathan Reeve JR337.5b12p281 11001200.

59. King John. Robin's loyalty to King Richard and opposition to John's attempt to usurp his brother's authority is a theme of many modern tales. © Jonathan Reeve JR1247b12p320 12001250.

60. & 61. Edward I, who as Prince Edward was primarily responsible for Simon de Montfort's defeat and death at Evesham. © Jonathan Reeve JR1245b13p388 12001300 and © Jonathan Reeve JR1246b13p436 12001300.

62. Simon de Montfort's seal. Eric Pedler by kind permission of the Kenilworth History and Archaeology Society from their booklet *The Great Siege of Kenilworth 1266* published in 1966.

63. Simon de Montfort's last fight at the battle of Evesham 4 August 1265. © Jonathan Reeve JR1249b12p337 12001300.

64. The dismemberment of Earl Simon's body after the battle of Evesham, from B.L. Cotton MS. Nero D ii, f. 177. Eric Pedler by kind permission of the Kenilworth History and Archaeology Society from their booklet *The Great Siege of Kenilworth 1266* published in 1966.

65. Kenilworth Castle keep, as it would have looked when de Montfort's supporters were besieged there in 1266. Eric Pedler by kind permission of the Kenilworth History and Archaeology Society from their booklet *The Great Siege of Kenilworth 1266* published in 1966.

66. Nottingham Castle, a reconstruction based on archaeological evidence and analogous architecture elsewhere. Barry Vincent, after Nottingham Civic Society by kind permission of Keith Branigan, University of Sheffield.

67. An eleventh-century archer. Archery appealed to all social classes, and Englishmen hunted and sported with the bow long before they used it to win great victories in the Hundred Years' War. © Jonathan Reeve JR251b11p152 11001200.

68. An eleventh-century Old English calendar showing agricultural scenes typical of the months between May and August. Roger Godberd, who was a gentleman-farmer when he was not causing trouble, would have been familiar with the work-patterns shown here. © Jonathan Reeve JR313b11p157 10001100.

76. Robin encounters the knight whose son has committed murder and who cannot afford to repay the money he has borrowed to save him. The story makes it clear that the outlaws are not opposed to entire classes in society – only to individuals within them who misuse their power. © Jonathan Reeve JR1403b75p156 12001300.

Also available from Amberley Publishing

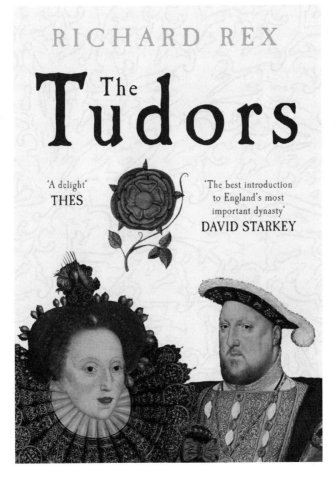

RICHARD REX

The Tudors

'A delight'
THES

'The best introduction
to England's most
important dynasty'
DAVID STARKEY

An intimate history of England's most infamous royal family

'The best introduction to England's most important dynasty' DAVID STARKEY
'A lively overview... Rex is a wry commentator on the game on monarchy' THE GUARDIAN
'Gripping and told with enviable narrative skill. This is a model of popular history... a delight' THES
'Vivid, entertaining and carrying its learning lightly' EAMON DUFFY

The Tudor Age began in August 1485 when Henry Tudor landed with 2000 men at Milford Haven
intent on snatching the English throne from Richard III. For more than a hundred years England was
to be dominated by the personalities of the five Tudor monarchs, ranging from the brilliance and
brutality of Henry VIII to the shrewdness and vanity of the virgin queen, Elizabeth I.

£20.00 Hardback
100 colour illustrations
320 pages
978-1-84868-049-4

Available from all good bookshops or to order direct
Please call **01285-760-030**
www.amberley-books.com

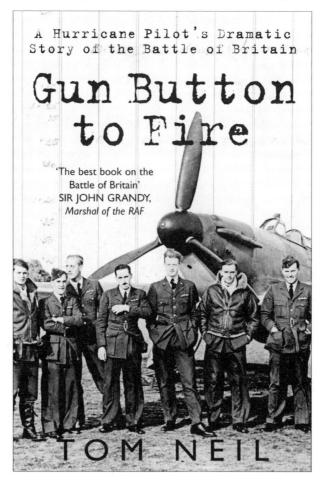

A Hurricane Pilot's Dramatic
Story of the Battle of Britain

Gun Button to Fire

'The best book on the
Battle of Britain'
SIR JOHN GRANDY,
Marshal of the RAF

TOM NEIL

*The amazing story of one of the 'Few', fighter ace Tom Neil who shot
down 13 enemy aircraft during the Battle of Britain*

'The best book on the Battle of Britain' SIR JOHN GRANDY, Marshal of the RAF

This is a fighter pilot's story of eight memorable months from May to December 1940. Nineteen years
old, fresh from training at Montrose on Hawker Audax biplanes he was soon to be pitch forked into the
maelstrom of air fighting on which the survival of Britain was to depend. By the end of the year he had
shot down 13 enemy aircraft, seen many of his friends killed, injured or burned, and was himself a wary
and accomplished fighter pilot.

£20 Hardback
120 Photographs (20 colour)
320 pages
978-1-84868-848-3

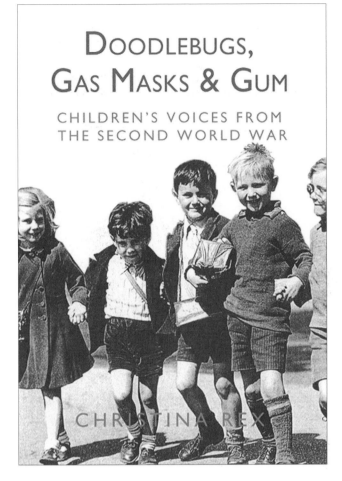

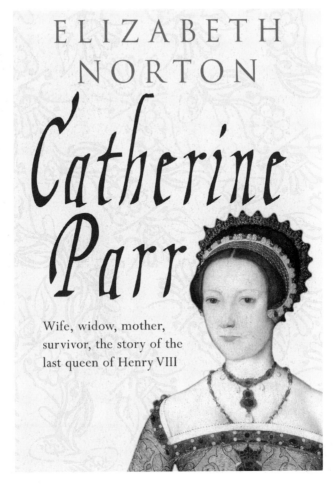

Also available from Amberley Publishing

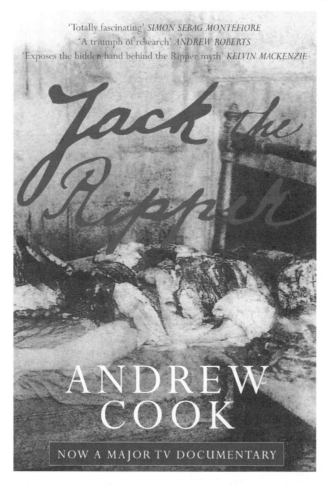

Finally lays to rest the mystery of who Jack the Ripper was

'Totally fascinating' SIMON SEBAG MONTEFIORE
'A triumph of research' ANDREW ROBERTS
'Exposes the hidden hand behind the Jack the Ripper myth' KELVIN MACKENZIE

The most famous serial killer in history. A sadistic stalker of seedy Victorian backstreets. A master criminal. The man who got away with murder – over and over again. But while literally hundreds of books have been published, trying to pin Jack's crimes on an endless list of suspects, no-one has considered the much more likely explanation for Jack's getting away with it... He never existed.

£18.99 Hardback
53 illustrations and 47 figures
256 pages
978-1-84868-327-3

Available from all good bookshops or to order direct
Please call **01285-760-030**
www.amberley-books.com

INDEX